Pearl's Diary

1906–1930

Pearl's Diary

1906–1930

The life and times of Pearl, Lady Montagu of Beaulieu

Editor E A Loving

First published in Great Britain in 2017 by

Beaulieu Enterprises Limited
John Montagu Building
Beaulieu
Hampshire
SO42 7ZN

Designed by Keith Miller

Maps by Battlefield Design

Set in Bembo and Gill Sans

Printed and bound in Great Britain by Hobbs the Printers Limited, Southampton

A CIP catalogue record for this book is available from the British Library.

ISBN 978-0-9523386-2-8

CONTENTS

◆◆◆

EDITOR'S ACKNOWLEDGEMENTS

Lord Montagu invited me to edit his grandmother's diary and produce a commentary on her life. Such was enormity of the task that we decided to concentrate on her early years and draw a line at 1930, just after the death of Pearl's first husband, John Montagu. His support, encouragement and practical help over the course of this project have been invaluable. James Crathorne and Gerald Cubitt have generously assisted with important information and photographs that would otherwise have been unavailable to me. I should also like to thank Ruth Binney for her editorial oversight, and Susan Tomkins for providing research help and making the resources of the Beaulieu Archives available. All photographs are from the Montagu and Cubitt family archives.

FOREWORD

♦♦♦

Pearl's mother, Clara Crake, and my grandmother, Violet Dugdale, were sisters. Violet's only son, Thomas, was my father and so first cousin to Pearl. Consequently Pearl and her sister, Gladys, spent much time when they were growing up at my family home, Crathorne Hall in Yorkshire.

Pearl had kept a diary from childhood and consequently the happy times spent at Crathorne are well documented. But the diary is also a remarkable chronicle of love and loss in the early years of the 20th century. It is a concise, factual, practical and down-to-earth account of daily life.

The diary also describes the highs and lows of great happiness and profound sadness that Pearl experienced as a young woman. Four years after the death of her fiancé, Harry Cubitt, in the Battle of the Somme in 1916, she married John, Lord Montagu of Beaulieu. It is impossible to exaggerate the success she made of her marriage to John. Pearl committed herself completely and wholeheartedly to John and his home. As a result theirs was a blissfully happy marriage, blessed with three daughters and the longed-for son and heir, Edward.

John's death in 1928 left Pearl with four young children and the management of the Beaulieu Estate. It was an enormous challenge but Pearl's courage and determination pulled her through and with the help of those around her she triumphed over tragedy. She steered Beaulieu through the difficult times of the Great Depression and the Second World War and so was able to hand the estate over to Edward Montagu on his 25th birthday in 1951. Her management had been a triumph, something acknowledged by her son who told me that he felt without his mother's stewardship of Beaulieu, the estate might well not have survived.

By the time Pearl died in 1996 she had 18 grandchildren and 23 great-grandchildren. Her obituary in *The Daily Telegraph* described her 'energy and delight in the moment', qualities that I well remember. She was an inspirational and influential person in many people's lives, including my own. To be allowed to share in Pearl's life through her diaries is both a privilege and a pleasure.

Crathorne.

yeo

MONDAY 1 [1—364] [**31 DAYS**
*Circumcision, Commonwealth Day
Stock Exchange Holiday. Bank Hol. Scot.*

Bitter east winds so as we
have colds mummy kept
us in, we wrote letters in
the morning & lied school
room Daddy started hunted

TUESDAY 2 [2—363]

rindy & cold so did not
ot out, cooked all the
fter-noon with Maude
Mummy enjoyed ball
Batty abt river much

THURSDAY 4 [4—361]

went for a walk with Diggl
in the morning & had
luncheon with Granny &
went to Mrs Cleavers
Xmas tree for baby & enjoy
ourselves awfully

FRIDAY 5

Wen
Mum
Lunc
Pierro
servents & Mrs Browne,
Captien

k with

came

we ac

came to

with mum

SATURDAY 6 [6—359] 1st Week
Epiphany

the eldens ba
I had a lot of presents as
it is my birthday, we walk
as far at the Gaity Theatre
with Diggles in the morning,

1
IN THE
BEGINNING

CHAPTER 1

IN THE BEGINNING

On New Year's Day 1906, in the Sussex seaside resort of St Leonards, a child began a diary with the words, 'Bitter east wind'. Pearl Crake was nearly 11 years old when she first put pen to paper on that cold winter's day and could not have foreseen that she was to keep the chronicle of her life for more than 90 years. She proved to be a remarkably consistent diarist and although there are breaks in the record, sometimes extended intervals, the narrative is always resumed, so mirroring her activities and concerns from childhood until her death in 1996 at the age of 101.

A personal record of this consistency and this duration is rare, especially as it takes place against the enormous political, social and technological changes of the 20th century. It is also unusual given the circumstances of Pearl's life and the person she was. By any measure, her diary is a document of considerable historical significance.

Pearl was the eldest daughter of Major Edward Crake by his second wife, Clara Woodroffe, and grew up in the final years of what has been described as Britain's imperial century when the country was at the height of its military and mercantile power. Presented at court to King George V and Queen Mary in 1913, she had the opportunity to experience society life in its final splendid exuberance before the cataclysm of the First World War, which robbed her, as it did so many women, of the man she had hoped to marry.

In 1920, at the age of 25, she became the second wife of John Douglas-Scott-Montagu, 2nd Baron Montagu of Beaulieu, the motoring pioneer and journalist. Their marriage was cut short by John's untimely death in 1929 leaving Pearl with four young children and the stewardship of the Beaulieu Estate, a heavy responsibility given the uncertain economic climate of the 1930s. That she managed to keep the estate intact for her son to inherit is testimony to her strength

A 1906 studio portrait of Pearl standing beside her younger sister, Gladys, the same year in which she began her diary. The picture was probably taken on 25 May when Pearl records, *We spent the whole morning at the photographers*. She noted that they could only go on the beach for 10 minutes that day, a restriction she must have found frustrating.

of mind and her courage. The circumstances of her marriage, her life with John, the birth of her children and her own experience of Beaulieu are all documented in the pages of her diary revealing a social order that had not changed substantially for some three centuries.

In order to understand Pearl, her life and times, knowing something of her own family and its origins is essential. For her, the family was always of first importance, its individual members forming the enduring reference points throughout her life.

From the very start, the diary shows the significance of the extended and complex network of relationships provided by her parents' families – the Crakes and the Woodroffes. From both her father and mother, Pearl inherited a distinctive cultural tradition and set of aspirations as well as a formidable mental and physical stamina which was to stand her in good stead.

The Crakes – climbing the ladder

Edward Crake's family had modest origins but for two generations at least it had been representative of the prosperous end of the rising urban middle-class, that vigorous and sturdy sector of the population that had begun to come to prominence with the industrialisation and increasing economic power of Britain in the late 18th century.

Edward's grandfather, William Crake, was born in London in 1787 when fundamental changes to both agriculture and industry were taking place that ultimately would transform the country. It was the year when the Committee for the Abolition of the Slave Trade was established and when the first convict shipment set sail for what was to become Australia. In 1803, at the age of 15, William was apprenticed to learn the craft of a painter stainer – a painter and decorator. He completed the seven-year apprenticeship but was only admitted to the Company of Painter Stainers in 1819 by redemption; that is on payment of a 'small fine' of 'Forty six shillings and eight pence'. It seems that he had contravened the rules by marrying during his apprenticeship, a hint, perhaps, of his determination and independence of mind.

Although a tradesman who could reasonably expect a lifetime of working for hire, William was evidently able enough and shrewd enough to take advantage of the building boom then taking place that was to extend London far beyond its medieval boundaries. His energy and drive were pivotal in the family history. He made his mark and his money as a builder and developer. In the 1841 Post Office directory he is listed as a builder, sharing the premises in Old Quebec Street in London with a young architect, his eldest son John Crake.

In this age of expansion William's London business did well, well enough to push his four sons and one daughter up a rung or two on the social ladder and, crucially, well enough for him to educate his sons; well enough, too, for him to become a person of standing in his community as a magistrate and, in 1854, to be appointed as a deputy lieutenant for the county of Middlesex. Eventually he moved from Old Quebec Street behind Oxford Street to 10 Stanhope Street, now Stanhope Terrace, on the edge of Hyde Park. Although his business was based in London, William also had property and connections in Hastings and seems to have divided his time between London and Hastings. His sea-front house in Pelham Place still stands.

Edward Crake's father, Vandeleur, was William's second son. He was born in 1816, the year after the Battle of Waterloo which finally ended the Napoleonic Wars, and was named for General Sir John Ormsby Vandeleur, a distinguished veteran of the French wars who at one point had sole command of the British cavalry on the field of Waterloo.

Vandeleur was a graduate of Jesus College, Cambridge and was called to the bar in 1841. He married twice, his first wife being Louisa Browne by whom he had three children – Winifred born in 1850, William born in 1852 and Edward Barrington born in 1854. Louisa died eight days after Edward's birth. In 1858, Vandeleur married again, and had another daughter, Alice, by his second wife Mary Delves. By 1861, the seven-year-old Edward was living in St Leonards with his father and stepmother, his sister and brother and young half-sister in a row of newly built houses collectively known as 'The Uplands' in a prestigious part of the town.

At this distance in time and with the minimum of documentary material, it is almost impossible to recreate the atmosphere of Edward's childhood home, but a most unexpected and unlikely commentator on the Crake family between 1858 and 1861 exists in the form of Edward Lear. Although he is now most remembered for his nonsense verse and limericks, Lear was principally a landscape artist. His diary for this period is a lively, sharp-eyed and occasionally sharp-tongued account of provincial middle-class life, and gives tantalising glimpses of the childhood environment of Pearl's father – a busy household with four young children.

It is evident from Lear's journal that the whole family – Vandeleur himself, as well as his parents, his sister and brothers – were all part of Lear's circle of friends: he saw them frequently when in England, both in London and Hastings; he corresponded with them, paid and received calls from them, and dined regularly with them. The impression gained from Lear's diary is of the Crakes as a close and sociable family presided over by the elderly William Crake.

The six semi-detached villas that constitute The Uplands still survive today, perched high in the town in the area known as Burtons' St Leonards after the architect, Decimus Burton, and his father, James. They are handsome, brick-built houses, with sash windows and quoins finished in dressed stone, unpretentious and comfortably proportioned dwellings with their own private access road set above and back from the public thoroughfare. Standing outside the Crakes' former home and looking along the frontages of the villas with their privet hedges and cast iron railings, there is almost no visual intrusion from the 21st century: it is not difficult to imagine Lear bustling along the gravel path to the entrance door at the side of the building for yet another musical evening, the children rushing out to play or Vandeleur strolling further up the hill to check the progress of the builders working on his new home.

Vandeleur was responsible for three massive stone houses built in Scots baronial style, complete with stepped gables and towers that were set in a commanding position at the top of the town where he lived for the rest of his life. The development was originally intended to be five houses but only three were built – it appears that the cost of such an ambitious project drained Vandeleur's finances, and even today in St Leonards he is remembered as the developer who 'went bust'. Although the houses are grand and imposing, it seems that modern residents find the huge rooms notoriously difficult to heat. It is hard to escape the idea that life might ultimately have been much more enjoyable for his family – literally and financially – had Vandeleur elected to remain in the relatively modest comfort of The Uplands.

In 1859 Vandeleur was commissioned into the newly formed 1st Company of Cinque Ports Rifle Volunteers as a lieutenant under the command of the local Member of Parliament. The 1840s and 1850s had been unsettled years. In England there was increasing social unrest with demands for reform. Elsewhere in Europe there was widespread political turbulence which resulted in the overthrow of a number of governments in 1848 – the Year of Revolutions. Although in general these movements were short-lived with a return to authoritarian rule, the result was to increase the fear of instability in Britain.

Deteriorating relations between England and France were not helped by the discovery that the bombs intended to kill Napoleon III in a failed assassination attempt in 1858 had been made in England. War between France and Austria in the spring of 1859 added to the anxiety with the possibility of a widening conflict. Many regular troops had been deployed to far distant parts of the British Empire and there was well-founded concern about Britain's ability to defend itself in the event of enemy action, or to keep the peace at home.

As a consequence Rifle Volunteers Corps were formed across the country to be called out in the case of 'actual invasion or the appearance of an enemy on the coast, or in the case of rebellion arising in either of these emergencies'. The seaside resort of St Leonards might well have been on the front line had the fears of invasion materialised. If Vandeleur was not to have the opportunity of seeing off the enemy on the battlefield like his military namesake, then he was certainly ready to play his part at home in the defence of his country. The sight of their father in his grey uniform with red facings and black braid as he went off to drill and take part in rifle-shooting competitions no doubt made a great impression on his children; they could hardly have been unaware of adult concerns about the political situation.

A rare image of Vandeleur Crake as he steps into the frame where his twin granddaughters, Winifred and Dorothy, pose for their photograph in about 1888. Their mother, Caroline, was the first wife of Edward Crake.

It is likely that these early memories of Vandeleur were in part responsible for his younger son's decision to pursue a military career. In 1873, at the age of 19, Edward Crake joined the Sussex Regiment which was a volunteer force. A year later he was commissioned into the Rifle Brigade where he served for more than 21 years before leaving in 1896. By the time that Pearl began her diary, he had been an officer on the Reserve list for ten years and was then acting as Brigade-Major in the Hampshire Voluntary Infantry Brigade.

In 1880, Edward married Caroline Dorothea Follett, the daughter of a barrister, Brent Spencer Follett, who in 1862 had become the first Chief Land Registrar of the newly created Land Registry. She died in 1891 in Switzerland leaving Edward with their eight-year-old twin daughters, Winifred and Dorothy. Three years later in a repeat of his father's matrimonial pattern,

Major Edward Crake was serving with the Rifle Brigade when he married his second wife, Clara Woodroffe, in the High Anglican splendour of St Paul's Church, Knightsbridge on 24 January 1894.

Edward (by now Major Crake) married for the second time. His bride was 26-year-old Clara Woodroffe, a distant connection of his first wife.

The Woodroffes — energy and enterprise

If the Crakes were typical of the emergent urban middle class the Woodroffes, by contrast, had their roots solidly in the rural gentry, a powerful and influential social group in England that had played a key part in its history for centuries. Gentry families owned land and had long associations with particular areas of the country; they also owned property in towns and cities, they were merchants, they were servants of the Crown, but generally speaking they were not members of the aristocracy. They sent representatives to Parliament, but usually these were members of the House of Commons rather than the Lords.

The Woodroffes were long-established in Surrey, with a network of property and connections extending into Westminster, Whitechapel and Chiswick as well as to the south Midlands. If the personal characteristics of Clara's father, the magnificently named George William Plukenett Woodroffe, were typical of his family, the Woodroffes collectively must have possessed enormous confidence, energy and curiosity. Even as a very young man, George, born in 1842, shaped his life with assurance and decision. Educated at Eton and Trinity College, Cambridge, he left Trinity after a year to buy a commission in 1860 in the Royal Horse Guards, a regiment that eventually amalgamated with the Royal Dragoons to form the Blues and Royals.

George's army career was brief but it was also extraordinary. He was a keen traveller and took the opportunity to explore large parts of the vast territory of Canada when he accompanied Lord Monck, later Canada's first Governor General, on a tour of inspection in 1862. Whilst on leave as a serving British officer, George was able to experience the American Civil War at first hand. He spent time with the Union Generals McClellan and Burnside in the campaign that led up to the Battle of Fredericksburg in December 1862. In 1864, he went as an observer to join the Headquarters Staff of the Confederate General Hood having run the Union Blockade of the southern States. He was with Hood in the lead-up to General Sherman's famous march to the sea, a prelude to the eventual capitulation of the south. Subsequently he travelled to see

Overleaf: The infant Pearl with her mother and family members at her christening in 1895. The central figure is her maternal grandfather, George Woodroffe. His wife, Alice, sits in the front row on the left. The two young girls are Pearl's half-sisters, Winifred and Dorothy. The two women on the left in the back row may be Pearl's maternal great aunts, Janet and Henrietta Townshend, while on the right are two of George and Alice's children, Pearl's Uncle Dick, then aged 16, and her Aunt Violet, who had married Lionel Dugdale in 1894. Violet and Lionel were to play a significant role in Pearl's life.

the defence of Richmond, the southern capital, by Generals Lee and Longstreet, eventually returning to Britain at the end of 1864. He was 22 years old.

Was this a personal enterprise by an enterprising young officer or had George been commissioned by the British government to report on the relative strengths of the two sides – the tactics, weaponry and logistics of a country on its way to becoming a world power – in what was the first large-scale industrial conflict? Whatever the truth, life back in England must have seemed rather dull by comparison with his experiences in North America and in 1865 George sold his commission. The following year he married Alice Maud Townshend.

In 1868 George, then still only 26, went into business with Henry Evans Gordon, setting up a firm of Madras bankers and traders, Gordon, Woodroffe and Company. This was the year in which his eldest child, Clara, was born. The business flourished, with the name of Gordon Woodroffe Ltd still surviving today in Madras as a manufacturing and freight forwarding business, the Indian and London branches having become independent companies in 1924.

Miss Alice Pearl Crake

Who was the young woman who was to be so important for Beaulieu? What was she like? Alice Pearl Crake, always known as Pearl, was born in London on 6 January 1895 at her maternal grandmother's house at 5 Buckingham Gate, a street running southwest from Buckingham Palace. She had one younger sister, Gladys, to whom she would remain close throughout her life. Although the diary focuses almost exclusively on events and activities rather than the expression of opinions and feelings, both the content and style are revealing, and the character traits are as marked in the child as in the adult. One very distinctive characteristic can only be described as 'groundedness', that is a strong sense of personal identity, of Pearl's place in her family, her circle of friends and the wider world; she was poised, a pragmatist and a realist, even at the age of 12 when recording the death of her maternal grandmother –

> *Dear Granny left us for ever early this morning, (Alice Maud Woodroffe née Townshend), so of course we did not go to the dancing class this afternoon but for a drive. We sang hymns after tea.* (8 NOVEMBER 1907)

She stayed often at her Aunt Violet and Uncle Lionel's home in Yorkshire, where she had the freedom to enjoy a range of activities not usually available to girls at the time including 'shooting at rafts down the river' as she noted on 9 August 1909.

By the time she was in her teens, Pearl had developed a keen sense of adventure and evidently enjoyed a physical challenge. Her diary entry for 19 March 1914, written while she was on her first visit to the south of France, is worth quoting in full –

A glorious day but very windy. Rosalinde Townley and I started at 9.30, picked up the two Amptill girls and Ursula Wright and then went by train to Roquebrune, three stations up the line. We all took our lunch with us, I carrying it in our satchel. We then walked about three miles all round to the back of the mountains of Roquebrune which rises 1113 feet straight up from the sea level. A beautiful red colour with five mag[nificent] peaks. We then started to ascend but only had a path for about the first 20 min walk, then we started real mountain climbing, finding our own way over boulders and rocks and mountain shrubs.

At last we reached the top of the shoulder and found it was impossible to get up peak 3, but after sitting on a ledge and having our lunch at 12, we managed to reach the summit of no 2 with difficulty, pulling and crawling on our hands and knees up the borders, by this time our skirts got so in the way so we turned them up round our waists under our jerseys and the straps of our travelling baskets kept them up, and we climbed for the rest of the time in just our knickers!! Much easier and more comfortable! But we were all so disappointed to find the cairn was on the next peak, and having got up so far, we all decided we must get to the summit, but there was deep ravine between the two peaks so we had to go half way down, and then all round number 1 peak and climb it from the further side.

At last at 3 o'clock we reached the cairn, having pulled ourselves up perilous places and oh! what a view we had, but we didn't sit up there long for fear of catching a cold, after being so hot. Just ate a tangerine each and carved out initials on the cairn and then started down. All our stockings were a sight to behold, we all had about 6 or 7 holes all up the leg. We had to walk all the way back to the village of St Roquebrune where the Wrights' car was waiting for us and we reached it at 4 o'clock, so we had been walking for 5¾ hours without stopping. Went home and changed and had tea at the English tea rooms.

The last sentence is typical and recurs time and again throughout the diary – the resumption of social norms is signalled by the fact of tea, an immutable ritual.

'To tea' was a verb in Pearl's lexicon – *I lunched and teaed at the Cavalry Club with Uncle L and Aunt Vi* (16 JUNE 1912) – and her days were structured around the fixed points of lunch, tea and dinner. Another very distinctive characteristic was a highly developed social sense. Pearl was an eminently sociable being, and this structure provided important opportunities for seeing family and friends, for inviting and being invited, part of the fabric of life right from childhood – *tea with Cecelia at Kensington Gardens and had great fun* (20 JUNE 1907). The pace of life was set to accommodate meals taken in an orderly fashion –

> *We did lessons by ourselves till 12 when the aunts fetched us for lunch. Mum, G[ladys] and I had dinner with cousin Alice at her club and then she took us to see Rigoletto at the new Opera House.* (30 JANUARY 1912)

If someone were to compose a soundtrack for the diary it would have to include the sound of tea being poured, of knives and forks being wielded and glasses being filled, together with the hum and buzz of polite mealtime conversation.

There are other typical usages. A favourite word for heavy rain is 'deluging' as in – *A deluging day, and strong SW gale* (1 NOVEMBER 1922). In 1927 she introduces the abbreviation 'CD' to describe someone being seedy or unwell. There are also many instances of 'danced hard', 'played hard' and 'shopped hard' in the early entries, reinforcing the overall sense of energy and action.

The diary also conveys a powerful sense of the enjoyment of life coupled with a sensory awareness. Pearl almost always notes the weather because the weather inhibited or enabled the activities of the day – *It poured with rain the whole day so did not go out at all* (26 APRIL 1907).

The phrase 'a lovely day' always refers to the quality of the weather rather than the emotional experience –

> *A lovely day. Mlle Grellou and I played 2 sets of tennis from 10.15 – my first this year.*
> (24 JANUARY 1920)

Pearl aged 15 in 1910 standing on the balcony of George Woodroffe's London flat in Queen Anne's Mansions close to St James's Park. The mansion block has since been demolished. Pearl's parents had rented a house in Onslow Gardens, South Kensington in the early summer that same year but Edward Crake died there unexpectedly on 8 July.

The scope of the diary is, however, far larger than domestic and social interests since it includes Pearl's accounts of, and responses to, events of national and international importance. These bring an immediacy to her record as with the description of the sinking of RMS *Titanic* in 1912 which reveals how communication problems compounded the anxiety of those waiting for news of family and friends –

> *For days in England we had very scanty and contradictory news of this terrible catastrophe till the Carpathia reached New York as all the news was through wireless telegraphy.*
> (14 APRIL)

An indication that her diary was an essentially private document is some of the spelling that appears in the early years. Although the content of these entries could have been read by a parent or governess without comment, it is unlikely that a phonetic rendering would have been allowed to pass uncorrected such as the entry for 23 February 1906 when Pearl writes – *We all went for a drive in showshible in the afternoon.* A sociable was a companionable vehicle, a horse-drawn carriage with two double seats facing each other and a hood that could be lowered allowing the occupants to view the scenery.

Right from the start Pearl demonstrated a knack of seamlessly combining small personal details with larger events. A very early example of this occurs in 1906 when she recorded the success of the Conservative Member of Parliament for Rye, George Courthope, in a general election when the Tories were heavily defeated otherwise –

> *Mr Courthope got in by eleven hundred today. Daddy was so pleased. Mummy came up and had tea with us as Dad was not in and she would have had to have tea all alone.*
> (20 JANUARY)

This ability to weave together very different information strands was to develop into a distinctive style that captured neatly the texture of Pearl's life, as well as the wider context of her time.

Her entry for 21 April 1926 is a particularly good example and manages to combine a pithy weather report, estate, family and personal information, as well as news of the birth of the future Elizabeth II. In just over a 100 words Pearl neatly conveys a flavour of public attitudes at the time, together with details of family gatherings at lunch, dinner and tea, and a comment on the quality of dinner –

A deluging morning. Clithero [the Clithero Estate Company, see page 168] *meeting at 10.30 – then dentist at 12.15. Great excitement as the Duchess of York gave birth to a little girl at 2 a.m. this morning. Guns were fired and a great crowd outside Bruton Street. I lunched at 21 with Aunt Netty, also Uncle Dick, Joan, Diana and Jack, all very excited over the baby sister, and also their time at Crathorne where they returned from yesterday. Shopped again and then had tea at 21 and Sylvia and Uncle Bill were there. John and I dined with Gladie and Cyril, Uncle Dick, Patience and Victor were there. Such a good dinner.*

The diary is essentially a factual record of people and places and activities. It was not intended to document Pearl's thoughts and fears and is in no way a reflective document. It also mirrors the attitudes of the time that later generations were to question.

If Pearl regrets a course of action, or chews over a decision, this is not recorded. She never agonises at length over her situation and this reticence makes her rare expressions of profound and raw feeling all the more poignant and powerful. She may have been pragmatic, she may have had mental and psychological resilience, but there is also the evidence of someone who was practised and socially adept at putting on a brave face irrespective of what was going on inside, and who had the courage to face life whatever it threw at her. As the years passed and the diary grew in volume, it seems to have developed its own entity – a resource that could be drawn on when necessary and to which Pearl turned almost as if to an old friend.

Throughout the diary, and throughout the years of her marriage to John which was to set the course for the rest of her life, Pearl herself provides the continuity and the voice, her appetite for life as apparent at 11 years of age as it was at 101 when, on 8 January 1996 after her final birthday party, she wrote, *Everyone thoroughly enjoyed my lovely party – lucky ME.*

SUNDAY 29 [149—216] 1st after Trinity

We went to early service with Mum this morning. Mum, G. & I went to tea with the Clarkes this evening. Nelle strained herself so stayed in bed till lunch to day.

MONDAY 30 [150—215]

Dorothy, Mlle, Joanes, G. & I left St Leonards by 10 — train & got to Queen Annes in time for lunch. We unpacked this afternoon, Mum & W. came by a later train, Nelle went to stay at her Aunts. We stayed up to dinner with Diggles.

TUESDAY 31 [151—214]

Mum, G. & I went to the dentists this morning & shopped.

2

MISS CRAKE

CHAPTER 2

MISS CRAKE

♦♦♦

If there is one word that describes Pearl's life for the first five years of the diary from 1906, it is peripatetic. She and her family appear to have had no settled home and were constantly on the move, a way of life that Pearl seems to have accepted without comment.

Although for those five years she gives her address as Canfield, St Leonards (Canfield was the name of one of the houses built by grandfather Vandeleur Crake at the Highlands), the family scarcely spent more than six months at a time there, instead circulating between Pearl's Woodroffe grandparents in London and her mother's sister, Violet Dugdale, at her house in Yorkshire, with occasional visits to the Dugdales' shooting lodge in Scotland. In December 1910, six months after the death of Edward Crake, Pearl left St Leonards and didn't return. The following year on 15 May 1911 she, her mother and sister went to 'our new house, 29 South St before lunch' – a flat-fronted Georgian building in South Kensington – where she lived until her marriage in 1920. This was to be the base for the final years of Pearl's education and the launch-pad for her entry into society as a fully fledged adult.

What was the reason for this nomadic existence with protracted visits to other members of the family? There are two possibilities to consider. One was that Pearl's mother wanted her two daughters to be brought up more within the orbit of her own family rather than that of the less well-connected Crakes. Pearl and Gladys were being trained and educated to be upper-class wives – effectively no other career options were open to them – and so moving in the right circles was vital. Clara's family was better placed to provide contacts and opportunities. Her younger sister (Pearl's Aunt Violet) had married well and lived in great style with her husband, Captain James Lionel Dugdale, at Crathorne Hall in Yorkshire. Lionel was responsible for the construction of the 115-room mansion, the largest to be built in the Edwardian period.

Pearl at the age of 17. She loved fashionable clothes and travelling gave new opportunities to shop. Her diary entry for 21 September 1912 when she was in Vienna is typical – *Mum and I went shopping … spent the entire morning trying to find a ball dress for me. At last tried on two we liked so decided to have them copied.*

Completed in 1906, this house formed the backdrop for much of Pearl's upbringing. Her cousins, Tom and Beryl, feature many times in Pearl's early diaries, Tom being almost a substitute for the brother that she never had – a valued companion and friend.

When Pearl began her diary her maternal grandparents, George and Alice Woodroffe, were living in a big house on Putney Hill. After Alice's death in 1907, George took a flat in Queen Anne's Mansions close to St James's Park, the 'QAM' of the diaries, a 14-storey residential block that was the tallest in Britain at the time, and which became a second home to Pearl and Gladys.

It is also possible that, for financial reasons, Pearl's parents were unable to sustain a separate establishment of their own at the level they felt was appropriate to their position in society, and so instead spent much time with the Dugdales or in London. A somewhat plaintiff correspondence survives from 1896, when Edward Crake was negotiating the lease of Denmead House in the village of Chawton in Hampshire. It is evident that basic repairs to the property were needed and some were still outstanding when Major Crake took over the tenancy –

> *My servant tells me when it rains, the top panes in the best bedroom, and in the drawing room let the water in very badly. There is also a pane half out in the room in the half landing.*

Requests for a verandah and extra fireplaces were refused. Edward also negotiated to lease some land for shooting and asked for a 'tennis ground' to be created. There is a sense of urgency expressed, with Edward asking whether Chawton Cottage (at one time the home of Jane Austen) could be let to him from 16 September until Denmead was ready. This request was granted. Clara was by then pregnant with Pearl's sister, Gladys, who was born on 30 November 1896. The family lived in Denmead until 1901 and so it is likely that Pearl's earliest memories went back to games on the 'tennis ground' at Chawton and her father setting off for a day's shooting.

'We went tobogganing with Dad'

Edward is a slightly shadowy figure although he features in Pearl's very first diary entry on 1 January 1906 – *Daddy started hunting.* He was obviously a lover of field sports and a keen fisherman sharing his interests with his young daughters – *After tea Dad took G and I fishing* (4 JULY 1908). He introduced them to golf – *Dad took Gladys and I out golfing this morning* (12 AUGUST 1909) – and evidently relished more childish activities – *It is still snowing. We went tobogganing with Dad this morning down Hollington hill.* (1 MARCH 1909).

But how robust was his health? He was 13 years older than Clara and as early as 1907 Pearl records what must have been a serious illness that lasted for some weeks – *Daddy is not a bit well today and the doctor came three times* (11 MAY).

The year 1910 marked a big change both for the country as well as for the 15-year-old Pearl. In May Edward VII died after a reign of less than ten years. In one of the last outings with her father, Pearl together with Gladys and Clara went up to London to see the King's funeral procession. Pearl was clearly impressed –

> *We got up at 5 o'clock this morning and left for the Berkeley Hotel at 6.30 as if we had gone any later the crowds for the King's funeral procession would have been too great ....*
> *It was a marvellous sight and took 18 minutes to pass.* (20 MAY)

Six weeks later, Edward Crake fell ill –

> *Dad had such pains all night. Dr P came soon after breakfast and said he had appendicitis so they got a nurse. We packed up this morning. We are going to QAM. At two another doctor came and decided to operate at 4.* (7 JULY)

> *We heard early this morning that darling Dad died at 3 o'clock in the night. He talked and knew everyone till 10 minutes before he died while asleep.* (8 JULY)

Neither Pearl nor Gladys attended the funeral. Edward Crake was only 56 and his death precipitated a huge upheaval for his wife and daughters.

Similarly, the death of Edward VII heralded a national change. He had given his name to an era renowned for its excesses – a man who had a whole-hearted appetite, literally and figuratively, for all that wealth and privilege could provide and who set the standard for a period of intense consumption and enjoyment. Although technically the Edwardian age had ended, the term is used generally to describe the time until the beginning of the First World War.

In extreme old age, Pearl joined that small band of people whose memories reached back to the extraordinary period of the first years of the 20th century. That world was to vanish and the structure on which it was based: the seemingly endless supply of cheap domestic staff who maintained the houses of those at the top of the economic pyramid; the apparently solid social

A group of cavalry and infantry officers stand outside a bell tent while on manoeuvres. Edward Crake is in the centre of the group wearing a white armband indicating that he was one of the umpires or referees for the exercise. The date of the picture is uncertain but the cap styles suggest a year of around 1902 when Major Crake was on the Reserve list.

order with its rules and values where each person knew his or her place; the world of imperial, political and cultural certainties. At this point, all seemed secure and stable and unchangeable.

More than 70 years later, Pearl remembered Crathorne in its splendid heyday presided over by Lionel and Violet Dugdale. Her aunt was 'much more severe' than her uncle, and the great house was run 'like a velvet-covered steel glove'. The staff quarters were strictly segregated 'with all the men on one side and all the girls on the other' to avoid, as Aunt Vi said, any 'trouble' in the house. There was always a footman at dinner but this was considered unremarkable and something that was taken for granted. One small room was used solely by 'the young boys who polished and polished and polished' the many pairs of Uncle Lionel's shoes. The teenaged Pearl noted all this and so gained a very clear idea of how things were done, and should be done.

This was the society that shaped Pearl's perceptions and aspirations and which gave her the first heady taste of the adult world. Like everyone else of her generation she could have had no idea of the changes in store, but simply accepted the way of life and all that it offered.

'Glorious bathing this morning'

After Edward Crake's death, George Woodroffe stepped forward to act as a support and companion to his daughter and granddaughters. His enthusiasm for sight-seeing had not deserted him and he was responsible for introducing Pearl and Gladys to the delights of European travel. The first overseas trip made by Pearl recorded in the diary is a six-week sortie to the northern French coast in July 1911. Her companions were Clara, Gladys and George, known as 'Diggles' to his family, as well as her mother's maid, 23-year-old Grace Haffenden –

> *Mum, G, Haffenden and I left the house at 8.45 for Victoria. We met Diggles there and went down to Newhaven by 10 train. We had wonderful crossing to Dieppe and arrived at 3 o'clock. We are staying at Hotel Royal. We have got such nice rooms. We went out and explored after tea.* (27 JULY)

Dieppe was an interesting mix in the early 20th century. It had become fashionable as a seaside resort a century earlier but from the 1880s had started to develop into a significant cultural centre. The presence of wealthy individuals with an interest in the arts had attracted a number of artists including Whistler, Sickert, Beardsley, Renoir and Monet for whom the Café des Tribunaux in the old market was a popular meeting place.

Soon after Pearl arrived there was a brief flurry of excitement, a reminder of how she grew up in a period of rapid technological innovation –

> *We were awoken at 5.45 this morning by soldiers lining up on the Plage as they expected Vedrines, he arrived here at 8.30. Had breakfast at our hotel and lunch too. He started off in his machine to Paris at 5.50 and got there in 1½ hours, wonderful!! All Dieppe saw him off. We took photos of him.* (4 AUGUST 1911)

The French aviator, Jules Védrines, was on his way back to Paris after a 1,000-mile air race. He had come in second, winning the consolation price of £200 as opposed to the victor's £10,000. *The Times* of 27 July was unsympathetic describing him as being in a 'state of great irritation' when he landed. Védrines blamed his defeat on bad luck although this was considered a poor excuse and briskly dismissed, 'If we analyse the bad luck we shall see that it resolves itself into inferior science and less excellent all-round education.'

Apart from this visitation, the six-week stay was uneventful. There were various excursions and sightseeing but essentially the sedate routine of middle-class English summertime life continued – meeting other English visitors against the familiar backdrop of regular churchgoing, tennis parties, lunches, teas and dinners interspersed with concerts. If she found this timetable at all monotonous, Pearl did not record her feelings.

'We shall not know you with your hair up'

The holiday in Dieppe and the subsequent lengthy European journeys were part of the educational system designed to fit Pearl and Gladys for the adult world. As Pearl turned 17 in 1912 while she was at Crathorne, she noted something seemingly quite insignificant –

> *My birthday …. I had my hair put up several times to see how it went.* (6 JANUARY)

At this date, all girls had long hair worn loose, until in their late teens they put up their hair and lengthened their skirts giving them a very different appearance. Pearl's was almost the last cohort to follow this convention. Her half-sister Winifred wrote her a postcard from Gibraltar where her husband Joss Egerton was stationed –

> *We shall not know you with your hair up – can you do it by yourself yet?*

This was the beginning of an important period of transition to adult life. For Pearl and others like her, the London Season was a key part of this change, a round of social activities originating in the 17th century when the landowning families came to London to socialise and take part in political life. For girls who were 'coming out' – the debutantes – namely those who were taking part in the Season for the first time, this included a formal presentation to the sovereign at court, a signal that these young women were now eligible to be married. But for Pearl in January 1912, this was some way off. The year ahead was a mixture of activities – educational and cultural – and approached with all her characteristic energy and enthusiasm.

On 29 July, Diggles, Clara, Pearl and Gladys left London to begin a long trip to Germany, southern Austria and northern Italy in what was to be the final years of the German and Austro-Hungarian Empires. Grace Haffenden again accompanied them as well as a courier, E. Schreiber. Schreiber (only ever referred to by his first initial and surname) was responsible for the details of travel as well as all the excursions. −

> *Mum and I went and did some shopping at Harrods after breakfast ... Went to Folkestone by a 2 o'clock train, had an awful crossing .... Got straight into the Basel express .... lovely scenery the whole way.*

Schreiber had evidently done his work well and the next two months were spent exploring an area of dramatic landscapes with a long and complex history − the borderland between Germany, Austria and Italy. This was a timely opportunity to witness life under the old regimes of imperial Europe that were to disappear in the upheavals of the First World War. The diary reveals how physically energetic Pearl and her family were: this was no leisurely holiday but a structured and purposeful journey of discovery. The weeks spent in and around the Dolomites are filled with accounts of expeditions that involved a great deal of activity for the whole party. The trip started in Innsbruck as it was to continue −

> *We went over the town this morning, went into Hofkirche and the Jesuite church. Very hot but windy. We went up the Hungerburgbahn plateau, 874 met high, in the mountain railway this afternoon. Had tea up there and then walked down.* (1 AUGUST)

> *Left the hotel at 9 and drove all the way by Zirl, Telfs, Obsteig, Lermoos, Reutte and over the boundary into Bavaria. We had lunch at the hotel at Hohenschwangau and then went up and went all over the Neuschwanstein Castle, built in 1869 by the mad King, Ludwig II, the interior is too beautiful for anything.* (4 AUGUST)

By mid-August they were travelling farther south in the Dolomites staying at the Miramonte Hotel in Cortina, a favourite spot for English tourists. A day trip was made over the border into Italy. Pearl's description is almost worthy of the English abroad in an EM Forster novel −

Overleaf: A party of tourists explores what is now the Stilfserjoch National Park in the Austrian Tyrol in a horse-drawn carriage at some time before the First World War. When Pearl visited the area in 1912, she described travelling along the hairpin roads of the Tyrol at altitudes of nearly 8,000 feet and the need to rest the horses at frequent intervals. This postcard is from her collection.

Left the hotel at 9.15 in a two horse carriage for Piere di Cadore in Italy, 15 miles. We were stopped at an Italian custom house and had to pay £15 deposit as our coachman had forgotten to bring his passport …. We started back about 5.30 and reached Cortina at 6.45. We stopped at the custom house to get the £15 back. (12 AUGUST)

By the third week of September the party had arrived in Vienna, at that date one of the cultural centres of Europe, where there was a mix of sightseeing and shopping as well as glimpses of European royalty –

After lunch we all went out to Schonbrunn in the tram [Schönbrunn Palace was the home of the then 82-year old Emperor Franz Joseph]. *We went over all the state rooms (very beautiful) and walked in the wonderful park with all the trees cut in avenues. Quite straight like tall yew hedges. We also saw the Emperor's own collection of wild animals in the park, there is no restriction at Schonbrunn, the public can walk wherever they like. The Emperor always lives at this Palace but drives into his Palace in Vienna every day. We saw him very well arrive back at Schonbrunn at 4.45 in a shut carriage …. Didn't get back till after 7 o'clock. King Manuel of Portugal* [Manuel II was deposed in 1910 and went into exile in England] *is staying here, he sat quite close to our table at dinner tonight. No one has been told he is here, but we recognised him.* (19 SEPTEMBER)

The holiday ended at Dresden with Diggles and Schreiber returning to England at the beginning of October, while Pearl, Gladys, Clara and Grace Haffendon stayed on.

After some two months of German language classes and an intensive round of opera going, including a solid introduction to Wagner, Clara took her daughters back home after just over four months abroad. Pearl was ready for the next stage in her life.

'My first dance'

Pearl arrived back in London on 1 December. There was evidently much to be done before she was ready to make her debut, and no time to lose. The next day preparations started –

Schreiber (far left), Gladys (seated), Clara and Diggles pose for Pearl outside the Hotel Austria on a day trip by car to the resort of Gmunden at the northern end of the Traunsee on 17th September 1912. The lake can be seen in the background. Ever the celebrity spotter, Pearl noted – *Both Duke of Wartenburg and Duke of Cumberland have large houses in lovely grounds overlooking the lake. We drove up to the door of both as we wanted to know if Princess Fredericka of Hanover was staying there …. A glorious journey and beautiful sunset. Went 60 miles an hour once or twice.*

In her early diaries Pearl often records joining her Uncle Lionel (above left) and cousin Tom on shooting or fishing expeditions. This picture may have been taken in the Scottish Highlands when the Dugdales stayed there in August 1909.

Shopped all the morning hard, dresses, coats and skirts (2 DECEMBER). Shopping took up most of the following two weeks, with Uncle Lionel assisting with a luxury that would have been unthinkable a decade earlier –

> *Uncle Lionel has very kindly written to say we may have his car for the week so we shopped all day. So nice dashing all over London in it. Had tea at aunts and then tried on dresses* (9 DECEMBER).

On Saturday 14 December Pearl and Clara went to Crathorne – Gladys was already there. A big house party was due to assemble for two balls – the first to be held at nearby Rounton Grange, the home of a neighbour, Sir Hugh Bell, and the second, Pearl's formal coming out ball, at Crathorne Hall –

> *A glorious day. Walked to the village and back twice this morning .... 21 of us went off in motors to Rounton to the Bells' dance. Uncle L, Diggles and Gladys stayed behind. This was really my first dance and I enjoyed it awfully, danced till 3.15.* (18 DECEMBER)

We got up in time ready to go in the car to the Rounton Meet at 10.30. Followed them for some time and then returned to lunch …. We had 7.30 dinner. The people for the Ball began to arrive at 9.30. Casana's band played too beautifully. There were about 400 people and it went off beautifully. We danced hard till 3.30. We did enjoy it so much.
(19 DECEMBER)

Pearl commented the next day - *Very sad it is all over.* But she was now officially an adult and free to dance all night if she so wished.

More guests arrived at Crathorne for the New Year, and there was yet another big party, this time in fancy dress —

We all dressed up for the Arabian Knight dress which began at 6 o'clock. We are 31 in the house for this dance, age limit from 8 to 78 with a few exceptions. Had procession and supper at 7.30 … they all had such lovely clothes. After everyone had gone at 10.30 we had another supper and then danced the New Year in and all sang Auld Lang Syne then we ended up with a two step. Everybody's doing it! We all perfectly loved it and it was such a pretty sight.

Despite these sophisticated entertainments, other simpler pleasures still had their place —

All went for a walk to the farm and slid down hay ricks etc till lunch. (31 DECEMBER)

The following year, 1913, during which Pearl was a debutante, was a whirl of social events, of having fun with old friends, and meeting new people. She was 18 at the beginning of the year. Lessons still continued — three hours on Monday, Wednesday and Friday afternoons, including cookery classes — but these were secondary to the business of taking her part in society.

In 1913, Pearl attended 18 balls and went to the theatre and cinema 24 times. Lunches, teas and dinners with friends and family away from home (not to mention holidays and weekends away) amounted to nearly 150. Pearl undertook 31 shopping expeditions, in addition to dressmakers' fittings. There were nearly 90 engagements and outings, including weddings, 'girls' teas', paying calls, ice-skating, polo at Hurlingham, race meetings at Ascot, Sandown and Epsom and the Eton v Harrow cricket match, as well as exhibitions ('did the Academy thoroughly'), extended weekend visits, two visits to Crathorne, to Scotland in August for the shooting and nearly three months spent travelling in France and the Pyrenees. There is a breathless quality to the diary for this year but nevertheless Pearl conveys the impression of someone who was more than able to cope with all that was required of her, including the demands of a presentation at Court –

> *We all went in one motor together to the Palace. We got there nice and early, so got lovely seats in the Throne Room. The King and Queen arrived at 9.30. Mrs Barlow Webb and Queenie Lewin and Leila went too, so after we had done our curtseys we joined them and stood together and watched the King and Queen and all their suite and the other Royalties and the Foreign Ministers pass through after all the presentations were over. Such a pretty sight. We all left about 11.15 – enjoyed it thoroughly. We all drove straight to QAM where I changed my dress, took my feathers out of my hair and then Mum and I went on to Lady Harvey's dance at the Ritz Hotel. Got home at 4 o'clock.* (7 MAY 1913)

Pearl's first Derby coincided with the action by the militant suffragette, Emily Davison, who stepped in front of the King's horse, sustaining fatal injuries. However Pearl was more concerned with the racing itself and the fate of the horses –

> *A lovely day. Uncle Dick, Mum and I trained down to Epsom Derby Day by 12.15 train and went straight to Uncle Lionel's box ... This is my first Derby, enjoyed it thoroughly. Quite the most unlucky and sensational ever witnessed. Mr Bower Ismay's Craganour favourite beat Aboyeur by a head, most exciting race. All so near at the finish. About 25 minutes later we noticed objections put up – the stewards decided that Craganour had barged Aboyeur so he was ousted, Aboyeur considered 1st, Louvois 2nd and Great Sport 3rd .... quite ½ hr before they settled it ....The King's horse Anmer fell by Tattenham Corner owing to a suffragette reaching out and catching the bridle – the jockey was badly hurt and the woman horribly trampled on and doubt she will live.* (4 JUNE)

'No English and Americans we are glad to say!'

Pearl and Gladys went to the Dugdales' shooting lodge in Scotland at the beginning of August 1913, and then at the end of the month, they, together with Diggles and Clara began another lengthy European tour. As before, they were accompanied by Schreiber and Grace Haffenden,

Violet Dugdale, Pearl's maternal aunt, stands with her brother Richard Woodroffe on the terrace outside Crathorne Hall, Violet and Lionel Dugdale's Yorkshire home. The photograph was probably taken by Pearl when a large houseparty assembled at Crathorne to celebrate her coming-out ball in December 1912.

This time they travelled down to south-west France on the border with Spain. Schreiber and Diggles had planned a varied trip to include both the beautiful scenery of the Pyrenees as well as the coast on the Bay of Biscay. It was a long and tiring journey –

> *We left the house at 9. Schreiber, who is going to be our 'courier' again this year met us at Charing X. Diggles joined us there in the carriage just before the train started at 10 for Folkestone. Had a wonderful smooth crossing.*

> *We had a terrible hot train journey from Boulogne to Paris, 80 degrees by thermometer. Arrived at 4.30. Drove to Hotel d'Orsay where we had dinner. Paris frightfully sultry and close. Schreiber and Haffenden went on by a 7.30 train but we didn't leave till 9 o'clock, our two trains joined at Bordeaux. We have lovely sleeping carriages and all went to bed soon after we started. The heat is so sudden. Mummy felt quite queer this evening.* (28 AUGUST)

> *Woke at 7.50, arrived at Pau ¾ late. Had a long stop at Lourdes …. Arrived at Pierrefitte at 10.35 instead of 9.30 and got in to the mountain railway for Cauterets and arrived at our destination in the Hautes Pyrenees at 12 and drove straight to our Hotel d'Angleterre. Have very nice rooms. Absolutely surrounded by mountains which are covered with trees of every sort, but the air is very fresh and light. A misty day so cannot see the view very well. Hotel is entirely full of French and Spaniards, no English and Americans we are glad to say!* (29 AUGUST)

The first part of the holiday was again a mixture of physical activity and sightseeing. Pearl's diary testifies to the way in which the trip was planned to make the most of each day with not an hour being wasted. Some of the expeditions were especially memorable and even inspired Pearl to occasional lyricism –

> *A glorious day. Left the hotel in a hired car from Pau at 10. Motored by Pierrefitte, St Sauveur to Gavani, 45 miles. A glorious drive, lovely views. Gavarnie is at the foot of the cirque, 4416 ft. …. Mum, G and I rode donkeys up to the Cirque to see the cascade which is really 5½ kil from Gavarnie, up very steep and rugged path … it took 1½ hrs to get there. Donkeys had to go single file. The Cirque is an immense cul-de-sac, a vast amphitheatre and above it tower five huge snowclad mountains, the crests of which form the frontier. The mighty walls are wept over by water from the melting glaciers.*

The highest cascade falls into the arena from a height of 1270 ft and the spray waved in the air like an ostrich plume. In summer there are only two weeping streams but in spring practically the whole of the Cirque is one fall. Rode back, had tea at Gavarnie and motored back. Reached Cauterets at 6.50. (2 SEPTEMBER)

Vigorous walking was a feature of the holiday –

Went for a short walk with Diggles before lunch. This afternoon Diggles, Schreiber, G and I went for a long walk without stopping for 2½ hours through the next village along the road on the other side of the river which leads to Spain, then we turned off on a footpath and came back on the road of the Val du Lys. (16 SEPTEMBER)

At the end of September the party arrived in at the fashionable seaside resort of Biarritz, some 22 miles from the Spanish border. After one unsatisfactory night in their pre-booked hotel Diggles decided to relocate the party to the very grand Hotel du Palais, once the summer residence of Emperor Napoleon III and his wife, the Empress Eugénie –

Arrived at 5.15 and drove straight to Hotel d'Angleterre. Have got very nice rooms. We four went straight out in the town and had tea at a café. Biarritz is frightfully full of Spaniards and Russians, practically no French and no English at all. Everybody looked very smart in the streets!! Explored about most beautiful shops, mostly branches of Paris and London shops, such as Mappin & Webb. (29 SEPTEMBER)

We were not very comfortable in this hotel last night as there is no nice place where we can all sit after dinner …. Went out soon after 9.30, walked right through the town to the other side. Saw the huge Hotel du Palais where King Edward always stayed. On the way back Mum and Diggles went in and asked about prices and rooms. They are quite full except 3 nice rooms on the 4th floor. After lunch Diggles decided to move from Hotel d'Angleterre to Hotel du Palais. H had to pack everything up again. We all went out and walked up to the other end of Biarritz …. Had tea at a confiserie which was full of very smart people. Have got nice though small rooms at Hotel du Palais which is a huge and magnificent place. Lovely lounges and rooms downstairs. (30 SEPTEMBER)

A brief trip over the Spanish border brought Pearl face to face with Spanish cuisine –

Left hotel at 9.15 … for a long run right along the coast into Spain to Ondarroa, a large and picturesque Spanish fishing town, snuggling in the natural bay which makes so good a harbour …. absolutely a world of its own, clothes of various colourings hanging out of all the windows of the high houses, fishing nets hanging over the bridge to dry …. Had the most extraordinary lunch … course after course of the most horrible and extraordinary dishes, Schreiber says we had great Spanish luxuries!!! As we don't know a word of Spanish, couldn't ask what dish was coming next – no menu. (9 OCTOBER)

At the end of October Diggles and Schreiber went back to London leaving the rest of the party in Paris for another month – again a round of sightseeing, the opera and shopping. There was also a disturbing brush with modern art at the Salon d'Automne, the annual art exhibition held in Paris which had begun as a response to the conservatism of the art establishment. In 1913 it included work by Roger de la Fresnaye and Albert Gleizes –

After lunch Mum, G and I went to see the Autumn Salon which has just opened. Room after room of ghastly cubist impressionists and futuristic pictures and as none of the pictures were named and there was no proper programme we hadn't the faintest idea what they all meant and were very pleased to have seen anything quite so eccentric and extraordinary but never mean to go near such a place again. (16 NOVEMBER)

Just before they left for home there was a strange incident with their maid –

We found Haffenden in an awful way as in the middle of packing she found that my mauve silk dress had been stolen from cupboard outside, this is the third dress since we have been here!!!! Mum was furious and went and told the Manager at lunch; afterwards he said he wanted to speak to her and said that he was sure we didn't know that ever since we had been at this Hotel, Haffenden had been seen continually going out at 11 at night and coming back at 7 in morning. Mum wouldn't believe it so went and asked her at once, and she owned she had! Of course Mum had to give her notice at once, we are all so terribly upset, we don't know what to do as have so explicably [implicitly] *trusted her and she has been such a wonderful maid for 3 years and of course we are all so fond of her.* (21 NOVEMBER)

Christmas was spent at Crathorne as usual. Pearl had a bad cold but recovered in time for the New Year celebrations. Her last diary entry for 1913 has an almost fairytale quality –

23 deg of frost last night on the 10 in of snow yesterday. A glorious day, brilliant sunshine and clear sky but still freezing hard …. We all stayed up and played Bridge and roasted chestnuts till after 12 to see the new year in. Great fun. (31 DECEMBER)

Pearl's photograph taken on New Year's Eve 1913 shows the façade of Crathorne Hall in deep snow. No one who took part in the celebrations at Crathorne that year could have had any idea of what lay in store in the months ahead.

SUNDAY 29 [149—216]   1st after Trinity

We went to early service
with Mum this morning.
Mum G. & I went to tea
with the Clarkes this
evening. Nellie strained herself
so stayed in bed till lunch
to day.

MONDAY 30 [150—215]

Dorothy, Mlle, Jones, G & I
left St Leonards by 10 — train
& got to Queen Annes in
time for lunch. We unpacked
this afternoon. Mum & W.
came by a later train. Nellie went
to stay at her Aunts. We stayed
up to dinner with Diggles.

TUESDAY 31 [151—214]

Mum. G. & I went to the
dentists this morning &
shopped.

THURSDAY 2 [153—212]

We left Queen Anne's soon aft
breakfast for 27 Onslow Gdns
house we have taken for 6 weeks
unpacked till 12-30 when mun
& I went to Claridges for lunch w
Aunt ... money
there ... hael Lyf
us th

FRIDAY 3

We d ... f ours
till ... nts fer
us to ... ent to
& have with Marie & Mel
the former has put her a f
& the latter has a chill
came & fetched us, she & Dad had
w ... at Cla

3

HARRY

SATURDAY 4 [155—210]   24nd Week

We did lessons till 11-1
then went to see ho
Melle was before lune

CHAPTER 3

HARRY

There is no hint in Pearl's pre-war diaries of any romantic attachment. If there was, she took very good care to hide it. But the years between 1914 and 1920 were to be defining ones for her and a test of her mental, psychological and emotional resilience – a toughening and maturing process, one that she could not have imagined and one that was achieved at a terrible cost.

The year after her coming-out ball in 1912, marking the point when she was officially admitted to the ranks of adult society, was spent enjoying the very best that life could offer thanks in large part to her Aunt Vi and Uncle Lionel, as well as to her own energy and a physical stamina that verged on athleticism. The year 1914 began in the usual way with Pearl as part of the family party at Crathorne. Then it was straight into a strenuous social programme interspersed with days spent walking and shooting. The entries for early January are typical of her life at this period. On her 19th birthday on 6 January she went to a masked ball in York –

> *Danced hard from 10 till 4.50 – the end. Didn't get in bed till 5.30.*

The next morning she played table tennis and went back by train to Crathorne. The following day she was at a dance at neighbouring Rounton Grange –

> *It was great and a lot of people we knew. Danced to the end and got back at 3.15.*
> (7 JANUARY)

That same evening she was back at Rounton with her cousin Tom where she *danced with the house party till 11.15 which was great fun*.

Many of the surviving photographs of Harry Cubitt show him with his terrier. In one taken by Pearl, possibly in 1916 when Harry was on leave from active service in France, he is shown standing on the terrace of his family home, a large Italianate mansion built by his great grandfather, Thomas Cubitt, on the North Downs in Surrey. Pearl came to know the house well, but later generations of the family found it too costly to maintain and it was eventually demolished in 1953.

On 16 February, Pearl, Gladys and Clara left Dover for a stay of nearly three months in the south of France, the haunt of the wealthy and fashionable who made a pilgrimage each year to enjoy the sun. The days there were similarly active, filled with tennis, sketching, shopping and, significantly, golf. On 11 April Pearl first mentions two new golfing partners –

> *Went up by the 9.30 bus and started playing golf with Miss Harman. Both Mr Cubitts – the eldest in the Coldstream and the younger just left Eton and is learning French at Versailles, joined us at the 9th hole and after that we had a foursome. Both are such nice boys, they have got a villa out here and live near the Barlow Webbs at Dorking and a house in London.*

The 'nice boys' were Harry and Alick, then aged respectively 22 and 20, the two eldest sons of Henry Cubitt, later to be the 2nd Baron Ashcombe and his wife, Maud, who were staying at the family's villa at Valescure. Harry was a lieutenant in the Coldstream Guards which he had joined in 1911 after leaving Eton. He was the eldest of six sons and, in the course of time, was due to inherit both the title and a 4,000-acre estate in Surrey acquired by his great grandfather, the master builder and developer Thomas Cubitt, who had founded the family's fortunes.

That meeting with Harry and Alick marked the beginning of a lifelong friendship between Pearl and the Cubitt family. It also marked the beginning of a highly important relationship for Harry and Pearl that took root in the spring sunshine on the golf courses and tennis courts of the Riviera ('Harry Cubitt and myself played some hard tennis'), and started to grow in the social life of London. The diary gives nothing away regarding her feelings at this point.

At the end of May she made her first visit to meet his family at their country house –

> *I am going to spend the Whitsun weekend with the Cubitts at Denbies. It is the most lovely place on the top of a hill 400 ft above Dorking and a drive of 2 miles. Mrs Cubitt met me in the hall and took me out to the tennis courts where all the party were playing …. Violet Long came and told me that Mr Cubitt couldn't bear seeing women's hands so everyone staying here has to always wear gloves – wash leather in the daytime and kid at night! Extraordinary idea!! The awful thing is that I haven't enough pairs of long kid, unless some come from the cleaners tomorrow by post and as it is Whitsun all the shops are shut till Tuesday. Anyway Violet Long says she will lend me some!* (30 MAY)

The season rolled on with balls and dress fittings, tennis matches and visits to friends. But as the summer progressed, events in central Europe began to intrude on the idyll and could not be ignored. Pearl was staying with friends in East Sussex when she wrote –

> *When the papers arrived we found that the Heir Apparent and his wife, Duchess of Hohenberg have been assassinated in the streets of Sarajevo, capital of Bosnia. Full account, it sounds too horrible – I expect Austria will make a great fuss about it. It all seems too sad for the poor old Emperor of Austria – and he has had such a sad life of it.* (29 JUNE)

Pearl first visited Denbies, the Cubitt family home, as a guest at a houseparty in spring 1914. Harry's parents, Henry and Maud Cubitt, are in the centre of the front row with Harry standing behind his father. The visit to Denbies was obviously a great success, with Pearl recounting on 30 May how the younger members of the party went down to the billiard room after dinner *where we could make as much noise as we liked.*

A month later back in London there was serious anxiety about the possibility of war. Dinner with Uncle Dick one evening turned out to be a very sobering occasion –

This morning's paper looks very grave. Russia is asked by Germany to explain her object of mobilisation, Austrians have taken possession of Belgrade which is reported to be in flames. Terrible panic in the City …. Bank rate has risen to 20% …. Uncle Dick was most interesting, but fearfully pessimistic. We all felt dreadfully depressed when they left. Of course, he was all through the Boer War and realises what war means. (31 JULY)

At this point, Aunt Vi was in Germany at a spa hotel and couldn't be contacted, but two days later she arrived back in London after a hair-raising journey across Europe –

Mum, G and I and Diggles went round and dined in the flat at Claridges at 7.30 to see Aunt Vi and hear all her accounts of the journey. None of the travellers ever thought they would be allowed through the frontier and she says their joy was untold on seeing the boat at Flushing. They were on board from 1 till 7 in the morning before she left as she had to wait for two riders from Berlin. The crowd on [round] her was too appalling …. She doubts ever seeing their luggage again as the boxes were piled up to the top of the station at Frankfurt and Basle as they just threw them out of the trains. (3 AUGUST)

On 4 August Britain declared war on Germany with immediate mobilisation. Pearl's diary entry for the following day was a characteristic mix of both the larger and the smaller pictures –

The British Ambassador leaves Berlin. Sir John Jellicoe takes supreme command of the Home Fleets and Sir John French of the Forces. Cousin Etta came to tea.

'This War is truly too awful!!'

At this point, the whole narrative of the diary changes from an account of debutante life into a record of the impact of war. Pearl signed up for a nursing course –

Miss West and I went to the Home Nursing lecture and practice again this morning. Just had time for lunch and then Miss West and I met at S Ken Underground and went by bus and then tram to York Mansions, Battersea to Miss Sebastian's flat where they are kindly teaching us bandaging …. We are all busy knitting every minute. (22 AUGUST)

The young men who made up Pearl's circle began to leave for active service in France –

Dick Lumley arrived just before lunch at 1 o'clock. He has taken a box at the Hippodrome for 'Hullo, ragtime!' So he took Gladys and I to it. We enjoyed it awfully …. We all think Dick is rather depressed and serious although he tried to be jolly. It is so difficult to keep off the war topic. We are really the last people he will see as he has said goodbye to his own people and he won't be up in London again. A car came at 9.15 for him to motor back to Aldershot. We all sent him off with every good luck. Oh! I hope he will get back safe! (17 AUGUST)

News of the first casualties arrived all too soon –

The first dreadful list of dead, wounded and missing was in this morning's papers from the battle of Mons, 10 days ago. Mr Tylee in the 15th Hussars who was staying with Aunt Fanny at Newbury when I was there for the Wells dance on July 25th, just 5 weeks ago, is dead. It all seems such a short time ago! And so dreadful. (3 SEPTEMBER)

Had a wire tonight to say poor Freddie Des Voeux has been killed in action. Feel sad for Lady des Voeux who is still at Frinton. (19 SEPTEMBER)

We saw poor little Marian Gough there, looking oh! so sad. John Gough in the Horse Artillery was killed just a fortnight after he went out and she had only been married 3 weeks. (20 SEPTEMBER)

Dick Lumley wrote to Pearl –

Had a long interesting letter from Dick Lumley written on the 24th, it was the 12th day of the Battle of Aisne and now it is the 22nd day and it is still raging. He says the German's artillery is marvellous but their infantry and cavalry not so good man to man as ours. They rely on numbers. Their infantry can't shoot for nuts. (3 OCTOBER)

Then Pearl had her first direct experience of loss –

I have got a long letter from Dick Lumley written on 16th. He seems to have been doing most dangerous and exciting patrol work lately, but so far they have only had 1 officer killed, Mr Ainsworth. He got my long letter 3 days before he wrote. He wants me to order him another pair of trousers and service jacket from his tailors to be sent out. (21 OCTOBER)

Oh! it is too awful, we found this cutting in the Times this morning. Dick was killed the day after he wrote to me that long letter I got only yesterday. It seems too awful and when I spent all yesterday ordering his new clothes to be made and sent out to him and I wrote a long letter to Mrs Lumley last night telling her everything I had done and she must have got it this morning and will have had the news privately for at least two days. I would have given worlds not to have written it and I wrote it so cheerfully too. This War is truly too awful!! It was only on August 17th he came up and spent the day here before he went out on the 22nd! One feels sometimes as if one couldn't bear it if it goes on much longer. (22 OCTOBER)

Even Crathorne fell under the spell of war, with Aunt Vi and Uncle Lionel setting up a convalescent hospital for troops there. Uncle Lionel donated two cars to the war effort –

Uncle L has offered Dr Shields his two cars the Daimler and Wolseley to do what he likes with to take the wounded from the battlefield straight to his hospital he is starting at the Carlton Hotel in the Champs Elysees. (6 OCTOBER)

News came of the scale of the losses and battlefield conditions –

Mr Arthur Hardy – cousin of John Hardy in the Scots Greys – came over to lunch. He is quite a boy and not long joined the Coldstreams. He went out with 1st Battalion which doesn't exist now – not an officer standing and only 38 men!! (22 NOVEMBER)

Uncle Dick arrived back this morning …. He was so interesting and told us of the horrors our poor troops are suffering with the wet and cold. After 4 days deluge they had 10 deg of frost at night and our men were standing up to their waists in freezing water. He saw 170 cases of frostbite. (24 NOVEMBER)

Pearl and Gladys made a weekend visit with Harry to Denbies in spring 1916 where tennis was the main focus of activities. Pearl recorded on Saturday 13 May, *After lunch we went and rolled the hard court and then played tennis till tea … Harry, G and I had great sets of tennis.* Pearl took this photograph of Harry and Gladys that same afternoon. A week later, all thoughts of tennis matches forgotten, Harry returned to the Western Front.

Pearl saw in the New Year of 1915 very quietly in St Leonard's –

> *Bryant* [one of Clara's maids], *Gladys and I wrapped in eiderdowns leant out of the window and first heard Christ Church ring the old year out, then the Parish Church struck 12 – then Christ Church and then it pealed the bells till 12.15 – so pretty and such a glorious night. Then we sat by the fire eating chocolates. Let us all hope and wish that 1915 will prove itself a happier year for all the world than 1914! And that this awful war will soon end!* (31 DECEMBER)

'It was too lovely dancing with Harry'

By the beginning of 1915 life for those not on active service had settled into a routine. As well as working for the Officers Families Fund that provided practical assistance for the families of men killed and wounded, Pearl also helped in the hospital at Crathorne which was up and running under the formidable leadership of Aunt Vi –

> *14 convalescent soldiers from Newcastle arrived today at 12.20. So of course Aunt Vi and all the Red Cross nurses were very busy. G and I went round and polished up all the brass. We watched them arrive from upstairs and then hurried back to the house. It is always rather an awful day – the first, Aunt Vi says as you have to find out what kind of men they are, and what their various ailments are – and if they are shamming!! She has to be frightfully firm and show them she won't have any nonsense.* (22 APRIL)

There is no mention of Harry throughout 1915 but he and Pearl were evidently writing to each other. There is a note at the back of her diary for that year regarding the gift of a purse for him at Christmas. Harry acknowledged the gift in a letter dated 29 December –

> *Very many thanks indeed for the Xmas presents, both the purse & the plums, both have arrived now. The plums in fact have arrived & disappeared.*

A total of five letters written by Harry to Pearl over the course of 1915 survive, the first dated 23 February. In one dated 30 October, just after the end of the Battle of Loos, Harry upbraided Pearl for being a bad correspondent, meanwhile apologising –

> *I am afraid this is a very dull sort of letter but I hope you will write again before I become a colonel or anything like that.*

In February 1916, Harry went on leave and the two finally met again. By now, Harry was 24 years old, and had been in France for some 18 months. Pearl was 21 –

> *Mr Greville came in to tea and Harry Cubitt. I haven't seen him since the Cross' dance on the Eton and Harrow night before the war; 19 months ago – what ages it all seems – he has been down at Denbies all his leave and just up for one night – he stayed with us till 5.50 when he went off to catch his train.* (10 FEBRUARY)

In May when Harry again came on leave, Pearl and Gladys went to Denbies with him –

> *Harry Cubitt arrived at 10.30 in his car and motored Gladys and I down to Denbies – a lovely run, arrived about 11.45.* (13 MAY)

Back in London Harry and Pearl went to a dance –

> *It was too lovely dancing with Harry again – he hasn't been to a dance since before the war – and really enjoyed it I think. An awfully good dance – knew everyone there. I loved it more than ever as Harry was there, he saw us home.* (15 MAY)

Harry returned to France writing to Pearl on 17 May – *I am now feeling very depressed at having to shake the dust of London finally from my heels, or rather tyres* – and the correspondence between the two continued. By now they were on first name terms. The time spent together in London had been a catalyst for them both, even though it appears that nothing had been said. A few days later on 21 May, unable to contain his feelings any longer, Harry wrote to Pearl –

> *You have my deepest apologies for what follows. I am more than sorry for doing it. In the first place because I have a horrible feeling that you neither expect it nor want it, and in the second place because I had never meant to do anything of the sort until we had finally settled matters with the Bosch. However what is the good of apologising for what one intends to do.*

> *What I want to know is, whether you could ever regard me as anything more than a friend. It seems years & years ago now that I first made up my mind to ask you some day, but when this war started I tried to forget all that sort of thing while it lasted, and have always abused all war weddings and engagements. That was all very well, but now*

that I have met you again, I simply can't help it, I must know whether there is any hope for me. Gossip damn and blast it, I loathe vague gossip, always brackets your name with somebody else's. For God's sake be kind Pearl and let me have an answer as quickly as you can. I don't want you to tie yourself down to anything at all simply say what hope there is for me.

P.S. I can't stand this letter now that I have read it through, it looks like a page from a third rate penny novel, but I can't help it, it must go.

Pearl's reply of 23 May was immediate –

I got your dear letter this morning and can't tell you how sweetly I think you've put everything. I am so very happy to feel that you really care for me. I somehow thought you

A rare photograph showing Pearl and Harry together, taken probably at Denbies, with one of Harry's brothers.

didn't and although we have seen so very little of each other the last two years, I always felt you were my greatest friend and now dear, it seems so splendid that we have found out our love for each other is real.

I know that I have always – inside – looked upon you as different from my other friends and now I know that no one I shall ever love as much. I felt so wretched the day after you left the other day, and it was then that I knew that I really loved you and that you made such a difference. Oh! I do so long to have a lovely long talk together – it seems all so difficult to write and one can't put into words – how one feels, as it never reads just the same!

Harry's letter of 28 May explained how he had hidden his feelings the last time he saw Pearl –

If I could only tell you what I felt like that night after I left you at South Street, after the second dance. I wonder the carriage had any unbroken glass left in it by the time I got home. I didn't sleep much that night. I am afraid that finished it with me. I [forgot] all resolutions to keep quiet till after the war. To begin with I thought that you didn't care a damn, that made it a thousand times worse. How the devil did you do it Pearl. I always thought up to now that I had a certain amount of self control, but I must have been wrong.

For Pearl who no longer had to conceal her feelings, the experience of loving and being loved in return was truly wonderful –

Went to the War Office and tried to collect my wits – after this morning's too thrilling news!! …. The red letter day of my life. I am so so happy – as although I have always inside me cared for Harry more than any of my other friends, I never felt he liked me any more than any other girl; even our last weekend at Denbies, he never gave me the impression of really loving me. (23 MAY)

Harry and Pearl agreed to keep their engagement a private matter for the time being –

It is too glorious. I got such a long letter from Harry by 1st post in answer to mine – I've had to wait ever since Tuesday, nearly a week!! It is such a dear letter and he is so happy – like me. We have settled to tell no one except his father and mother and then

Diggles, Aunt Vi and the Aunts – not till August when he comes home on leave again and we can have a lovely long talk. (29 MAY)

A letter from Harry, written on 1 June to Pearl's mother, is evidence that Clara approved the engagement and had written to Harry. Harry felt his behaviour in effectively proposing to Pearl without the knowledge of her mother was out of order, as the tone of his letter reveals, but nevertheless he is completely unrepentant about his feelings for her –

My dear Mrs Crake
I think that it is more kind of you than I can say, particularly on paper, to write me a letter such as you have. To begin with I feel that even in ordinary times I should have had no business to write to Pearl while you knew so little of me …. I have always been one of the loudest criers down of war engagements throughout the whole war. I hope you will some day forgive me, but I am afraid I lost my head. I was afraid I should when I heard that Mother had asked them to stay at Denbies for the weekend; I always felt after that night I came to tea at South Street that another meeting would be fatal & the only thing to do would be to avoid each other till the war was over. All this I am afraid sounds disgustingly weak and what good can apologising do after the deed is done. As it is I can only pray with many others that this cursed war will finish before people expect & if I survive it I hope that some day I may make Pearl so happy that you forgive me for all my present misdeeds.

But Harry never had the opportunity to atone for his 'misdeeds'.

On 21 September while Pearl, Gladys and Clara were enjoying a holiday at Eastbourne, Clara received a letter from Henry Cubitt, Harry's father as Pearl recorded that day –

Heard news of the death of my darling Harry.

Mummy broke the awful news to me that my own darling Harry has 'Gone' – Oh! how can I bear it! Dear Mr Cubitt wrote Mummy the bravest most wonderful letter which she got by the 5 post. They only heard this morning from Alick (the 2nd brother in the 15th) who had seen one of the Coldstream men, who saw my darling hit 70 yds from the trench and the Dr says death was instantaneous. It was on the morning of last Friday 15th when they all made the attack. Oh! it is too too awful. Poor Mr & Mrs Cubitt, they idolised him. I only wrote to him today – there must be quite 6 he has never got. A week tomorrow and we only just heard. Stayed in bed for dinner. Absolutely heart broken.

Aware of the enormity of the loss and and the impact on Pearl, Henry Cubitt had written rather than send a telegram in case, as he said, 'the telegram got into wrong hands'. Their affection for the young woman whom they regarded as their future daughter-in-law is evident, *Poor dear Pearl she is so young to have such a blow & our love goes out to her.*

Pearl's diary is testimony to the sensitivity and kindness of Harry's parents towards her –

Mum heard from Mr Cubitt to say he was up in London and would come and see me at 2.45 this afternoon …. Mr Cubitt had a talk to Mum 1st all about my darling, but I think he was rather anxious about how I should take it, so he talked to me more about the other brothers and then more ordinary conversation – he was too charming as usual. (6 OCTOBER)

Mrs Cubitt came to see Mum and I …. Oh! it was too lovely seeing her and having a long talk about my darling – it is 3 weeks today since we heard the awful news. I simply can't get over it, she gave me the most lovely diamond ring which had belonged to my darling's grandmother, and which his father and mother had kept for him to give his wife one day, and now they have given it to me. Oh! it is too dear of them and I just love it. I will always wear it and it will help comfort me and although I can't wear it on my left hand I can always think of it as what would have been my engagement ring. (12 OCTOBER)

Pearl's final diary entry for that year is poignant –

We all went to bed very early tonight, somehow this year I could not socially have seen the New Year in. 1916 has been the happiest and ended by being the saddest I've ever had and I hate to feel it ends and slips away tonight. This year will be for ever the Red Letter year of my life – for just 3 months and 3 weeks I was the happiest girl there could ever have been – happy in the great love of the best of men and bravest of soldiers …. I am left now, just the saddest girl with the memory of my darling, his precious letters and his photos. (31 DECEMBER)

'It seems so hopeless!'

In the same way that Pearl was reticent about her feelings for Harry until his letter in May 1916, so for the most part she remained silent about her grief. Part of their tragedy was that Pearl and Harry never met as acknowledged lovers, and in this regard Pearl's sense of being cheated must have been all the greater.

In the early days of 1917, it seems that Pearl was operating on two levels, outwardly energetic and bright but inwardly in great pain that was almost overwhelming at times –

> *Cyril's birthday party has been such fun and I enjoyed it all while it lasts, but it makes me feel so sad and I miss my darling Harry more and more. Last night I felt too miserably wretched when I went up to bed.* (31 JANUARY 1917)

Her grief was compounded by the deaths of Harry's next two brothers – Alick aged 23 in November 1917 and Hugh aged 22 in March 1918. Hugh's death coincided with the retaking of the Somme by the Germans which meant that Harry's grave was now in enemy territory. That same month Pearl took up a post as a clerk in Military Intelligence, a department of the War Office, noting on 25 March, *The hours are fearfully long 9.45 – 7.* She was assigned to section MI 1A that dealt with intelligence records..

The war drew to its slow and bloody conclusion. A week after the Armistice was signed in November 1918 Pearl went to visit Harry's parents at Denbies. Henry Cubitt had succeeded to the title as the 2nd Baron Ashcombe the previous year on the death of his father. Pearl now referred to Harry's mother as 'Cousin Maud' –

> *Cousin Maud is looking very well but Lord Ashcombe says she has felt rather tired out this last week – as we all have been feeling – Peace is very trying to a lot of us.*
> (16 NOVEMBER)

In 1919 a memorial chapel to Harry, Alick and Hugh was dedicated in the Denbies Estate church. The occasion brought conflicting and painful emotions –

> *It was all very grand and sad, but one felt so proud of ours who gave their lives for us all. .... I felt pretty lonely tonight when I went up to bed. I just want my darling Harry more and more. Can't he ever come back. It seems so hopeless!* (10 AND 11 JUNE 1919)

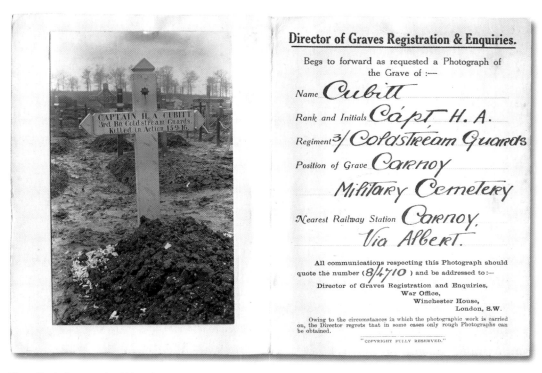

The official photograph of Harry's grave with its battlefield cross. Pearl was distraught when the photograph of herself that Harry always carried with him was returned to her after his death. She had hoped it would be buried with him.

The culmination of the year was a sad pilgrimage to France with Harry's parents in October to find the graves of the three brothers. In common with many others who were able to make the journey to the battlefields, they wanted to know the place where those they loved had died. Harry's was the only grave that could be clearly identified –

> *The Ashcombes have taken out a trowel, bulbs, forget-me-not plants and an oak cross. We took a little while to find our darling Harry's grave – they are all so overgrown and this cemetery so unkept …. We sickled all the grass and dug through all the soil before we planted the bulbs and then collected white chalk stones and put them all round and erected the oak cross at the foot, as we did not like to take away its own cross though it is damaged by a shell. The grave looked so beautiful when we left – and we longed to have been able to tidy all the others up too.* (11 OCTOBER)

They saw for themselves the impact of war and the environment which the three young men had experienced. It was only 11 months since the end of the fighting –

> *Fearful desolation and destruction …. Saw quite the worst devastation at Chaulnes – nothing has been done to tidy up here and everything was awful – shell holes, wire, shells, tin helmets etc – all German. Fearful fighting round here. Through Rosieres and onto the main road and home through Villers-Bretonneux. We have seen far worse devastation today. Ghastly everywhere.* (12 OCTOBER)

> *Today we are going to Bourlon Wood near Cambrai to try to find trace of where Alick is buried …. Just one vast desolation. The ground so churned up, like the face of the moon …* (13 OCTOBER)

Back home, Pearl found that her beloved grandfather, Diggles, was in failing health, unable to give Gladys away at her wedding to Cyril Cubitt, a distant cousin of Harry's, which took place on 10 November 1919, the day before the first Armistice Day. The timing of the wedding must have been especially hard for Pearl who needed no reminder of all that she had lost –

> *At 11 AM the maroons went off all over England and there was a 2 minute's silence in remembrance of all the brave silent dead. Some of us don't need such moments for thought but it is a grand idea.* (11 NOVEMBER)

All seemed to be changing. Towards the end of the year, there was yet another loss to be borne –

> *Aunt Netty told me at 8 this morning that our darling Diggles passed away while unconscious at 10.10 last evening. He suffered no pain and did not know he was going to die, which is a great comfort and relief to us.* (8 DECEMBER)

The old order had passed.

In 1919 Pearl, together with his parents, visited Harry's grave in the cemetery at Carnoy in France. The original cross had been damaged in the fighting and so they added a second cross at the foot of the grave. The shelling had been so intense that nothing remained of the village of Carnoy itself except for a few fruit trees.

AUGUST, 1920.

12.50 p.m. SATURDAY, 7th.

Wrote letters hard till 11. when I had to try on at Madme Buttons for last time; I am glad to say — dashed round getting final odds & ends before Tuesday. Little Looie arrived before lunch. she is putting up at Mrs Peels, to be with us till over our wedding. she Mummy & others helped arrange our presents at 25 Belgrave Sq. all this afternoon evening. Gladie lunched & sat I sat peacefully in Thurloe Sq garden until V brought Lionel & Berys to it in the — SUNDAY, 8th. —with us after

SUNDAY, 8th.

10TH SUNDAY AFTER TRINITY.

MATTINS—1 Kings xii (Genesis xxviii, v. 10 to v. 18); Romans viii to v. 18.
EVENSONG—Deuteronomy viii v. 15; St. Matthew xxi to v. 23.

Wrote letters hard till lunch. Went in a taxi to Claridges, & then went on to lunch with Aunt V. Berys & Uncle Lionel to Cavalry Club — essie & Dorothy lunched

AUGUST 1920.

MONDAY, 9th.

I went to Harrods & had chyrop... & manicure done & heaps of odds & ends till lunch. My darling John arrived at 1.30 from Bexhill. He dropped crowds of presents at 25 Belgrave Sq. ... was so nic... introdu... ...ive. At 3.3... we we... ...sents ...ooks ... brides... turned ... on their wreath ... had a wonder... ... She & V... came up ... today. John had to dash back to office at 5 & return... at 6.20 — very tired & took me back

TUESDAY, 10th.

Our Wedding Day the day of our (John & my) life. Aunt V. & ...ho... went round to 25 Belgrave Sq to se... to my presents & arrange jewelry furs. I came down to lunch half dres... at 12.40 with ...oo..., Miss Hamilto...

4

A PERFECT AND WONDERFUL DREAM

CHAPTER 4

A PERFECT AND WONDERFUL DREAM

◆◆◆

At the dawn of 1920 Pearl was almost 25 and there was nothing at this point to indicate what the future held for her. She was one of the thousands of young women whose hopes of personal happiness had been destroyed on the battlefields of the First World War. The immediate post-war period was a bleak time and not just for her personally –

> *The horizon is far from clear and the prospects for a peaceful year not too promising both internationally and industrially but one must hope for the best.* (1 JANUARY)

Among the books she read that month was John Buchan's novel *Mr Standfast*, which was first published in 1919. Set in the First World War, it is a tale of spies and subterfuge, a fast-paced narrative. It also provides the setting for the meeting between the hero, Richard Hannay, and his future wife, Mary Lamington, a Voluntary Aid Detachment (VAD) nurse who is less than half his age and who possesses beauty, intelligence, courage and energy.

It is tempting to speculate that the some of the characters in *Mr Standfast* were at the back of Pearl's mind when she left England on 14 January for an extended visit with her mother to the south of France. Certainly she could qualify as a Buchan heroine with her youth, courage, energy and physical attractions. Like Mary Lamington she was fair-haired and blue eyed. Like her, she had been a member of the VAD and like her she was both intelligent and resourceful. The war years had given Pearl opportunities to undertake work otherwise denied to women in her position providing her with structure and companionship. She would have understood all too well Mary Lamington's assertion that … *women aren't the brittle things men used to think them …. the war has made them like whipcord.*

A studio portrait of Pearl taken by the society photographers, Bassano, who described themselves as 'Royal Photographers'.

There must have been a very painful sense of déjà vu when she and Clara arrived in St Raphael, this time without the recently married Gladys. The diary is relentlessly upbeat –

> *Madame Brunel delighted to see us again and same hall porters and we have the same room as in 1914. Excellent food at dinner tonight so all looks so nice and clean.*
> (16 JANUARY)

The following weeks were filled with walking, tennis, and socialising as the number of English visitors increased. Pearl took up golf again, although this brought back memories –

> *This is the first time I've played since 1914 on these links. There are only 9 holes now instead of 18 and during the war they cut a road right through them. This is quite the hottest day we've had – it was too hot in the middle of the morning. It seemed so funny holding a golf club again – I've forgotten absolutely what to do! This place does remind me so of my darling Harry, we met out here and the last time I played was with him. I remembered so well the exact place where we were introduced!* (3 MARCH)

On 17 February there were new arrivals at the Hotel Beau Rivage –

> *Lord Montagu, Major & Mrs Limby, and Mr Archie Marshall (the author) came to stay today by car.*

John Douglas-Scott-Montagu was then aged 54. A motoring journalist and transport expert, he had inherited the title of 2nd Baron Montagu of Beaulieu together with the Beaulieu Estate in 1905. His first wife, the former Lady Cecil Kerr, had died the previous September after 30 years of marriage. He had decided to include a visit to the south of France as part of a motor trip to Vienna and Budapest where he was due to meet an old friend. Captain HER Widnell, who joined the estate staff in 1918, provides a good picture of John at this point in his life —

> *In figure Lord John was very well proportioned, perhaps slightly under the average height, with a strong, active, well-built muscular body .... The blue eyes, alert*

I'll put on uniform to have a new photo done for you, John Montagu wrote to Pearl on 10 June 1920, the day after they became engaged. He was first commissioned in 1886 into the 4th Volunteer Battalion of the Hampshire Regiment. In 1914 he took the 7th Volunteer Battalion to India. Four months later he was co-opted on to the General Staff at Simla as Inspector of Mechanical Transport where his specialist transport knowledge was put to good use.

expression, the slightly reddish hair of the true border Scot, combined with a healthy complexion all pronounce the outdoor man, par excellence …. Perhaps the feature that struck a stranger most strongly was his charming and engaging manner.

John only stayed in St Raphael for a few days, but almost immediately he began to feature in Pearl's diary –

Sat with the Montagu party after dinner – he has kindly offered us his car tomorrow afternoon when they are in Monte Carlo. (20 FEBRUARY)

At 2 Mum, Miss Arbuthnott and I went for a drive in Lord Montagu's car, through Ste-Maxime and on to the old fortress town of Grimaud, we climbed right to the top of the old castle and took photos – had tea at Ste-Maxime and got back at 6. It was too lovely. Mum and I dined at Lord Montagu's table. (21 FEBRUARY)

A gorgeous day, the Montagu party and us had great photography in the garden this morning before they set off to motor to Nice. (24 FEBRUARY)

But John Montagu had noted Pearl, and noted her carefully. At the back of his tiny engagement diary for 1920 there is the following cryptic description –

Blue grey eyes
Fair hair
25 yrs old
5 ft 4-6 ins
No money
Good temper

This makes complete sense as a description of Pearl at the time she met John. Is the note calculating, or just a practical male approach to finding a suitable mate? A vivacious and good-natured young woman capable of adapting to the way of life at Beaulieu would be well worth considering as a wife.

In the same way that John was hoping to meet someone whom he could contemplate as a second partner, so Pearl was also hoping to encounter a possible spouse. None of this was overt, but it was understood. The rules of the game were clear. But at this stage Pearl did not regard John as husband material — indeed initially, Clara thought that she herself might be the object of John's interest. As Captain Widnell noted in his memoirs —

… it was generally expected that he would marry again, and indeed rumour had it that several ladies had certain hopes.

At the end of April Pearl and Clara returned to London. Pearl had spent more than three months in France where she had rediscovered old haunts, and explored new ones. She had walked, played tennis and golf, gambled at Monte Carlo, been sight-seeing, shopped, and watched the flamboyant French tennis champion, Suzanne Lenglen, play in a tournament. Back in London, the remorseless social round was resumed — lunches, visits, matinée performances, shopping, teas, dinners and dances. But John Montagu had plans, and less than a week after her return home Pearl and he met up once again —

At 8.15 Mum and I dined at the Berkeley with Lord Montagu and Sir A Kingston Fowler. We had a charming dinner. He was very interesting. He then took us round to his rooms in the old house in Pickering Place [off St James Street] *in the 19 Hundred Club. It is too attractive, everything so old.* (5 MAY)

At the beginning of June Pearl visited Beaulieu for the first time. She was feeling exhausted having been at a dance the night before —

Called at 6.30 — very sleepy as did not get to bed till 3 AM. Mummy and I got to Waterloo at 8.45 — Aunt Vi and Beryl and Uncle Bill arrived at same moment! We all went down in one carriage of the special train to Southampton at 9.10 run by the Royal Mail Steam Packet Co. (Owen Phillips) to have a private cruise on their big liner Almanzora …. A lot of fellow passengers we knew. Arrived at the wharf at 11.15. Met Lord Montagu by the gangway …. We sailed right down Southampton Water and along the Solent — so pretty. After lunch we all spent on various decks again looking through

Overleaf: Beaulieu Abbey had been founded by King John early in the 13th century and granted to Thomas Wriothesley in 1538 at the Dissolution of the Monasteries. The former abbey gatehouse was converted into a dwelling which became known as Palace House. In 1872, Lord Henry Scott, John Montagu's father commissioned the architect Sir Arthur Blomfield to undertake a substantial remodelling and enlargement of the building.

glasses till we arrived back at 3.40. All the others had tea on board and went back to London by a special at 4.25, but at 4 Lord Montagu motored Mum and I to Beaulieu and got there in time for tea ... after tea we were taken all over the ruins of the Abbey – too lovely – absolutely dead to the world by dinner – have never felt so tired .... Beaulieu is quite beautiful. (4 JUNE)

I did not wake till 12!! So tired from yesterday. A lovely day .... At 3 Lord Montagu had the big fishing net out on the river as the tide was coming in – it was such fun seeing it pulled in, they did it twice and we caught quite a lot of mullet and brill.

Then we all went down by car as far as Buckler's Hard – the dear little old ship yard where the last of the wooden ships and Nelson's Illustrious etc. were built – a fascinating little place. There, we got into Lord M's motor boat and we came back to Beaulieu by her. After tea, Lord M took Mum and I and Sir Thomas Troubridge, a tour in the car all round his houses he has built over his property – all too fascinating, all old oak and full of his old furniture. (5 JUNE)

Mummy and I went to early service in the beautiful old Abbey. Then Lord Montagu, the Thornycrofts and we went at 11. Such lovely singing and a beautiful service taken by the dear old vicar. Such a lot of people come to this old Abbey on Sundays and all the nice people who live in Lord M's houses .... Lord M gave me a lovely bag from Vienna today with a crystal and diamond clasp – too lovely. (6 JUNE)

'The most vital question'

Two days later Pearl went to hear John speak in the House of Lords – the last time she referred to him in her diary to 'Lord Montagu' –

Got up a little late and then went and shopped a bit till lunch .... at 4, we 2 went into the Stranger's seats of the House of Lords to hear Lord Montagu speak on 'low flying aviation' ... and then Lord M came and fetched Mum and I and gave us tea and then

A formal portrait of Pearl taken probably two weeks before her wedding when she notes on 27 July 1920 that she went *to be photographed for Vogue.* That same evening there was a dinner in honour of Pearl and John at the Royal Automobile Club (John had been one of its founders) at its luxurious purpose-built headquarters in Pall Mall.

The tickets for the chairs hired by John when he proposed to Pearl in Kensington Gardens on 9 June 1920. She kept them on her dressing table for the rest of her life. Later John told her he had refrained from proposing to her at Beaulieu in case her response was influenced by the beauty of the surroundings.

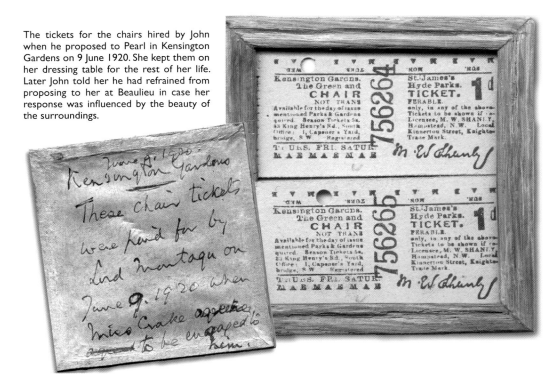

showed us all over the House of Lords. Later we drove Mummy back to South Street and he and I went on in the taxi and got out at Kensington Gardens.

We then went to sit near the Round Pond for ages, I had a feeling what was coming! Apparently he has been desperately in love with me ever since we met at St Raphael in February and had told Mummy, but of course she had kept the secret! I was absolutely ignorant and never guessed a thing – all the time I was at Beaulieu – till the last morning. It is wonderful to think a man of his age can be madly in love with me – when I haven't ever given him the slightest encouragement. He says he will give me everything in the world I want and devote his whole life to me – of course, I told him about my darling Harry and how no-one can be the same to me – and how I cannot yet love him the same way as he loves me, but he was so sweet and understanding and said he thought and dreamt of no one but me! Of course I am completely bowled over as I never even thought of him till Monday – except as the charming person who was always too sweet to me, it is all so extraordinary to think of me marrying a man of 52!,[sic] *but I must admit he is quite one of the youngest people I have ever met as he is so energetic. We thrashed everything out and I think he will make me very happy — everything will be for me and that wonderful Beaulieu.* (9 JUNE).

In accepting John's proposal, Pearl was characteristically straightforward about her feelings and, no doubt, about what she wanted. From now on her life was to be centred on John and Beaulieu rather than on London society. The courtship was brief and to the point — there are no references to dancing with John as Pearl had danced with Harry but instead detailed descriptions of the serious business of transforming Miss Crake into Lady Montagu, complete with all the appropriate accessories. She was not only becoming the wife of John Montagu but taking on the role as châtelaine of Beaulieu. She had seen many of her contemporaries — including her sister and half-sisters — pass into married life and so she was familiar with the rituals of preparation that accompanied the change in status. Now at last it was her turn, and she was determined to enjoy every moment —

Found Dorothy [Pearl's half-sister] *at South Street when I got back. She was so excited about my news. John came to fetch me at 7.30 and then at 8 he and I went off to dine with Louise Shennan in her dear little old house in Gilbert Street — our first dinner out together and we had such fun ...* (15 JUNE)

The preparations started immediately with a visit to a London jeweller —

At 3.30 Mum and I met John at Heming — the family jeweller in Conduit Street, he had all his family jewels out — some lovely things — the lovely pearl and diamond tiara suits me so well, also a darling little light diamond head band etc. John and I chose one or two pendants we wanted to sell, also the 3 large pearls, dropping from Holbein Cross, and I am going to have the money worth added to my pearls, which will be lovely. He gave me today a gorgeous diamond pendant heart — as an engagement pressie and with it came some beautiful words which he wrote for me. (16 JUNE)

An important part of the preparation was the marriage settlement, in effect a pre-nuptial agreement, the terms of which were to ensure that Pearl had adequate financial resources both as a wife and in the event of John's death. The settlement also allowed for any children, including a male heir. A document dated July 1920 outlined the proposals —

It is now proposed that Lord Montagu shall charge the Beaulieu Estate with a jointure in favour of Miss Crake should she survive him of £1,000 per annum to be increased to £1,500 per annum from 1st January 1930. Miss Crake is also to be given the right to live in or occupy which ever of the residential houses on the Estate, other than the principal Mansion House, she may select free of all rent. Lord Montagu will covenant to pay her £300 a year as pin money during his life.

Meanwhile there was shopping to be done and another visit to Beaulieu –

Frightfully busy writing letters, putting off engagements etc. till 10.30 when John came for me in a taxi. We dashed off to see the dear Aunts for 5 minutes then went to Duvelleroy about fans, then to Revillon about a fur coat he is giving me – then to ... Floris where we bought scent and powder, then to Orton's where we saw more fur coats .... joined John at Waterloo. Bertha [Pearl's maid] came down by same train – but Mum came by 6.30. I was introduced to 2 of the inspectors and then taken up to the footplates of the engine and introduced to Tom Wilson, the driver – a great friend of John's, they were all too sweet to me, then at Southampton West I was introduced to Lady Helen Whitaker, perfect dear, in her Girl Guide Commissioner's clothes – we travelled as far as Beaulieu Road together. We had a wonderful drive to Beaulieu, looking quite wonderful with June sun shining across the river by it – the first time John and I have come together .... I was so happy .... A gorgeous evening and we shall never forget it – our first at Beaulieu. (17 JUNE)

Pearl's second visit to Beaulieu included a tour of the village and the school, a well as decisions about arrangements and alterations to her future home. There was also a private service of Holy Communion led by the vicar which had a special significance for Pearl –

Had breakfast in bed and appeared at 10.15 – then John and I started our tour of village. He introduced me to every person we met in the street, and took me into every shop, agent's office etc. and then to the schools where John told all the children! They were all too sweet, they just adore him and meant to love me – it will take me ages to remember all their names, then we went all over the house, kitchens etc. I have chosen the little oak panelled room next to the drawing room to be my boudoir and John is going to knock a hole through the wall from his room to the room Mummy had – which will be my room – too delightful as we shall have our own bathroom etc. (18 JUNE)

John and I met at 8.45 and we went off to the beautiful old Abbey church, the dear old Vicar gave he and I a beautiful Communion service all to ourselves – our first – it was very perfect and I felt my Harry was blessing me. After breakfast I went round to see the servant rooms to choose two rooms for my maid. (19 JUNE)

This sense of receiving permission from Harry to marry another man was important for Pearl. John was the physical antithesis of Harry – of medium height and fair in contrast to Harry's dark colouring and considerable height. John was also old enough to be her father, a man with confidence and experience of life, not a young man so reserved he could not speak his love even in the face of acute danger and possible death. Nowhere in his surviving letters to Pearl does John mention Harry. For neither Pearl nor John was this first love, but rather a contract which was to form the foundation for a different kind of love and fulfilment. Despite the difference in age and experience they shared a common bond in that they had known both the joy of intense love, and as well as the anguish of loss. A few of Pearl's letters to John during their engagement survive and, in writing to him, she reveals the extent of her unhappiness in the years since Harry's death, and her joy in being with John, feelings that never found expression in her diary –

I want your love so badly – I've been a very lonely person since my sister married and it was hard seeing her so happy. (13 JUNE 1920)

It is evident that John was strategic in his wooing – he set himself to win Pearl. He introduced her to the context of his life, his home, the estate, his interests, his friends, his family, his work and then, after possibly as few as ten meetings with Pearl, he proposed. Years later, Pearl recalled –

My darling nearly proposed to me looking over the forest by Culverley but he told me he refrained as he thought that it was unfair amidst the glory of his own home, so the following Tuesday 9th of June, we became engaged in Kensington Gardens near the Round Pond! (27 AUGUST 1930)

John's expression of love for Pearl was unequivocal when she accepted his proposal as his letter of 9 June explains. He also had found life lonely –

My darling,
You have brought Heaven very near to me today. I woke this morning anxious – oh so anxious – as to my fate. I felt I must ask you the most vital question a man can ever

ask a woman, and what is more tell you how deeply I had come to love you with my whole soul and body. Ever since S. Raphael I have thought more and more of you by day and night, and you have in a sort of spiritual way been with me all the time. I have often prayed God to give you to me, and to make me everything a man should be to the purest and most beautiful Pearl on earth. Only last Sunday when you shared my hymn book I felt a thrill I can't express in words at your being next to me, and singing with me. You're just 'all the darling there ever was' as my friend Rudyard K. says.

As Pearl noted that day, *'Mummy says she has never seen such devotion'.*

It seems at this stage that Pearl's feelings were somewhat different. Still mourning Harry, she had seen swathes of young men of her own generation cut down before they had had time to taste life. Marriage to John would give her a chance to be mistress in her own home, a position within a community, and the focus for a man's affection. John was all too aware of this but he also hoped that her feelings would deepen as he wrote to her on 20 June –

… the memory of your eyes tells me still what I may be to you later on …. I am well content to wait for the fullness of your Love, praying that God will make me worthy of you, and feeling happy indeed that already I see the coming of a love light in your eyes.

Aunt Vi had suggested that no public announcement of the engagement should be made before September, the first anniversary of Cecil's death, to avoid any adverse comment about the speed of the courtship. But matters changed when John's brother-in-law, Harry Forster, was appointed Governor General of Australia. He and his wife, Rachel, John's sister to whom he was close, were leaving in August and so the wedding date was set for 10 August just before their departure.

But there was one hurdle to be overcome before the wedding. Pearl had been diagnosed with an 'adhered appendix' which needed removal. This was a risky procedure in the 1920s and given that her father had died after surgery for appendicitis there must have been considerable anxiety. On Monday, 21 June, the operation was carried out at her mother's house in South Street –

At 2 pm on Tuesday 10 August 1920, Pearl left her mother's house in South Kensington for her wedding at St Margaret's Church. Lionel Dugdale took her to the church and gave her away. As a member of the House of Lords, John was entitled to be married at St Margaret's which had been the parish church of the Palace of Westminster since the 17th century.

Lovely long letter from John before 9, so I was able to write little note before operation. 9 o'clock I went down to Mummy's room, where all was ready for the op. Parkie, Crisp English, Hysdale, Barcroft were all there – also my two nurses, Lambert and Harmer. Shook hands all round then they put me out quickly. Came round at 11 but dozed all the rest of the day. John came and just kissed me for one moment in the afternoon.

John visited daily when he was in London. The period of enforced rest while Pearl convalesced provided some respite from wedding preparations and a chance for privacy and peace.

Every morning a little cardboard box arrives with fresh verbena and roses from Beaulieu .... John came at 4.45 and we had tea together, and he sat with me till 7.30. We were very peaceful – he in a comfy chair ... (28 JUNE)

Back in Beaulieu, John reported on the progress of the building and renovation work taking place at Palace House –

Everything goes well here. They are doing your bedroom now, and the grate is out and the fireplace being made .... 4 rooms upstairs in the servants quarters are being got ready and in fact are practically finished. The new windows downstairs in your boudoir and door are well under way the grate there is out and the wood burning arrangements being made too.

In fact the nest is looking promising for the two birds, or shall I say Beauty, and the poor old devoted Beast who worships her. (15 JULY)

After convalescence in Brighton Pearl returned to London where both the wedding preparations and the social round intensified. Pearl was evidently still feeling the effects of surgery –

Crowds of lovely presents have arrived for me. I then rested this afternoon – and then at 4.45 John came and fetched me and he and I went to the garden party at Buckingham Palace together. We met a lot of people we knew and John introduced me to so many people. I got quite addled. He made me sit in a chair and brought people up to me!!, and then I had my shooting stick when I walked about – it was so nice going about with John

Pearl was attended by seven bridesmaids on her wdding day including John's younger daughter, 10-year old Elizabeth, her cousin, Beryl Dugdale and a friend, Juliet Glyn. Uncle Dick's four-year-old son, Jack, was one of the two pages.

for the first time since we became engaged, and we were so happy. Came back and rested and then John came to dinner – had a lovely evening together. (22 JULY)

John and Pearl were gradually introduced to other members of their respective families. John's cousin was the 7th Duke of Buccleuch who had married Lady Margaret Bridgeman in 1893 –

Cousin Etta and Aunt Henrietta came at 4.30 especially to see John – he arrives about then – then he and I went to tea with the Duchess of Buccleuch at 2 Grosvenor Crescent – she is so charming and a cousin of John's … (26 JULY)

Pearl made one more visit to Beaulieu before the wedding –

We all went to church in beautiful Beaulieu Abbey this morning. John and I and Elizabeth sat side by side. Lovely day …. At 4.30 all the guests, 100 in all, arrived on the lawn, just the near neighbours living on Beaulieu Manor – to meet me – all too charming. We had tea in the dining room – such a crowd …. Had a wonderful evening with my John. (1 AUGUST)

Pearl returned to London. She was now in the home straight for the wedding –

Wrote letters hard till 11, when I had to try on at Madame Burtons for last time, I am glad to say – dashed round getting final odds and ends before Tuesday …. Mummy and others helped arrange our presents at 25 Belgrave Square all this afternoon and evening. Gladie lunched and she and I sat peacefully in Thurloe Square gardens. (7 AUGUST)

Wrote letters hard till lunch. Went in a taxi to Claridges and then went on to lunch with Aunt Vi, Beryl and Uncle Lionel at Cavalry Club …. a most lovely summer day at last. Went at 3.30 to 25 Belgrave Square to see all John and my presents beautifully arranged in the two lovely rooms there – they will make wonderful rooms for a reception. (8 AUGUST)

My darling John arrived at 1.30 from Beaulieu. He dropped crowds of presents at 25 Belgrave Square…. At 3.30 we went to 25, the presents look so lovely. John and I said a touching farewell as lovers and he went of to dine with the Forsters. All very tired … went to bed fairly early. My last night in my little girl's home. (9 AUGUST)

Our Wedding Day. At 1.10 Madame Marte's two dressmakers arrived and dressed me in my wedding dress and lace veil forming my train – all Mummy's lovely old Bruxelles lace, and tulle veil and orange blossom …. We found a huge crowd at Westminster in front of St Margaret's, arrived at 2.15 to the moment. My bridesmaids all looked so pretty and the two darling pages. Church packed – it all seemed so beautiful and over so quickly. My darling John was looking so smart – when we were up at the altar we held each others hands which gave us such a wonderful thrill. Dear old Mr Powell married us so beautifully, and said a few wonderful words. Cousin Henry Ashcombe, Uncle Harry Townshend and Uncle Lionel, Duke of Buccleuch, George Montagu [9th Earl of] Sandwich, Tommie Troubridge and Harry Forster signed the register. We met a host of photographers as we came out of the West door – then my John and I (as man and wife) hereafter drove off in Mrs C Johnstone's car to 25 Belgrave Square. We had to go through more photography …. and then the reception …. My John and I left the reception at 4.30 and went to 53A Pall Mall to Col Beville's flat where we had tea.

The whole of our wonderful wedding day went off too splendidly – only over too quickly. Tommie Troubridge, Jane and dear Junard saw us off at Waterloo, 5.30, we had a wonderful time. About 30 more photographers to take us while giving favours and presents to the railway staff and Arthur Jacomb, the engine driver and great friend of my John's. Gave more favours at Southampton West and Brockenhurst. Teddie [Stephens] met us with car. Had a wonderful reception at Beaulieu, first at Manor Gate, and then we had to get out of the car and after a few words were said and I was presented with another bouquet in front of quite 400 village people, John and I marched behind the band, followed by all the people – flags everywhere and the Mill bridge beautifully decorated, then under the Archway of Palace House, more people and the Girl Guides and Brownies were formed up. I showed them and thanked them for the lovely bride's bouquet they gave me, then we said goodnight to them – such a wonderful reception, is too marvellous. John and I had dinner about 9 (our first together in our new home) as we had to change. So blissfully happy – may I for ever make my darling John the best of wives and happiest of homes.

It all seems a perfect and wonderful dream as yet – that we are really one at last.
(10 AUGUST)

☽ 2.13 p.m. *WEDNESDAY, 10th.*

Our wedding day, but the day told John that to go up to London for the day — so we really kept it yesterday. Mother & sent us such a charming wire. also always Geoffry Mark's. Elizabeth went off to a cricket match. mummy & I went up to tea with Mrs Heckstall Smith in her little cottage on Bunkers Hill, miss Campbell & miss Hewlett were there too — we had an amusing tea in the hut.

THURSDAY, 11th.

Elizabeth & miss Knott were fetched by the Poole's car at 12 — & went over to lunch at Lepe — before their boys cricket match, Eliz: didn't play — but watched. at 3.30 Mrs Martin & Miss Langford Brooke

FRIDAY, 12th.

Sonia & Rollie Cubitt had a daughter yesterday — we see in to-day's "Times". How proud Cousin Maud will be! Tommie & John went to shoot duck after lunch ... started to pour ...

5

BLISSFUL AS MAN AND WIFE

... with young ... sister ... about him — Mary is so affectionate ... does hope she is really ... Major Heckstall-Smith, Tommy

SATURDAY, 13th.

John took a sandwich lunch & went off at ... to trawl the river — they got in time for tea, having caught a few plaice etc; & a horse fish afterwards John & ... went up in the car to Calverley ...

CHAPTER 5

BLISSFUL AS MAN AND WIFE

◆◆◆

On her wedding day, in common with millions of other women before and since, Pearl made a solemn vow 'to love, to cherish and to obey' her husband. In her case, however, there was a significant difference: she was both marrying John as well as taking on a commitment to a place that was not only dear to him but was also the key to his identity. Ultimately, that same place would become part of her identity also. The nature of her previous life with its requirement for flexibility, discipline and organisation, for the ability to socialise and to make the best of things, as well as for sheer physical stamina and determination, had in effect been a form of apprenticeship. She was well prepared for the role she was to play as John's wife. Pearl's arrival at Beaulieu had enormous significance for the estate. In turn, the responsibilities that awaited her there and the events of subsequent years were to focus her formidable energies and to provide an environment within which her gifts and qualities could flourish.

Pearl first saw Beaulieu on a June afternoon at the start of a weekend's visit when she first began to realise what John's intentions might be. The weather conspired with John so that Palace House in its tranquil setting was presented to best effect in the summer sunshine. Right from the time of his proposal that took place shortly after that visit she knew how important his home was to him, writing on 9 June 1920 that *everything will be for me and that wonderful Beaulieu.* Pearl became part of a system that was in many ways a relic of feudalism where land ownership was a measure of status and influence and where, ideally, that land should be held by successive generations of the same family. John had chosen as his second wife a woman who, although she was not in a position to contribute material wealth, would, if all went well, provide the long-desired male heir and thus ensure the continuity of ownership and title.

The first weeks of marriage were spent mostly at Beaulieu as Pearl settled into her new home where she was able to observe her husband at close quarters in his preferred habitat. Many of the excursions recorded by Pearl were taken in the company of Teddie Stephens, John's chauffeur –

John and Pearl in the gardens of Palace House, with John's dog Bess, in spring 1922.

Palace House, Beaulieu, Hants. My Home, Our Home from August 10th 1920.

We are oh!, so happy – blissful as man and wife. Spent a lazy morning – I didn't go down till 12. A perfectly heavenly day – still and hot – the first real summer day since June for all of us. A photographer has been waiting for ages in front of the house, so we had to let him take us. Masses of photos and accounts in all the papers today of our wedding. Had tea at 4.30 after resting and then motored to Buckler's Hard and John, Teddie and I went down to the river and across the Solent to Newtown, Isle of Wight. Absolutely dead calm and gorgeous evening; we sat on the shore on the island. Got back at 9. The lorry turned up having left London at 12 today with all the wedding presents. We have them put in the Hall but are not going to unpack them yet. Speak [Pearl's maid] *is getting beautifully straight – and my bedroom is looking lovely with all its splendid old Chippendale furniture.* (11 AUGUST)

Another heavenly day …. heaps of good photos came by post …. After lunch we rested and sat in the garden this evening and wrote. Oh!, so happy. (12 AUGUST)

We and Teddie motored to Buckler's Hard at 3 and got in to the motor boat and went right down the Solent as far as Allum Bay (nearly to the Needles) a wonderful day and so still and hot, except at the strong race near Totland Bay. We had tea in the boat and then just landed at Totland for a little. (14 AUGUST)

Dull day but warm. We went to church at 11, first time together as husband and wife in our beautiful Abbey Church. Talked to a lot of people – who all congratulated us …. Then my John and I sat in two comfy chairs and he read Kipling to me. At 4.30 we motored over to Lepe to tea with Harry and Rachel Forster – heaps of people were there and they were all so surprised and pleased to see us. They sail for Australia on Saturday …. Such a gorgeous evening … fished in Hartford Hole [a favourite location on the Beaulieu River]. *John caught 2 trout. Got in at 9.40!!* (15 AUGUST)

Wrote letters till lunch and after then rested a little, then we motored over to Beaulieu Road and to a spot near Culverley on the Forest where John and I had sat on 7.6.20 while out otter hunting and where I first guessed he cared for me!! We were really sentimental!! The heather everywhere is looking too lovely. Dined at 7.15 and at 8 we motored to Hartford Hole and fished. (16 AUGUST)

On 17 August, a week after their wedding, Pearl noted, *We and Teddie motored to Buckler's Hard, and then got in the motor boat, took Jim and Ernest Thomas with the rowing boat and prawn net in tow and we went down to the mouth of the river.* Jim Thomas had the title of 'Lord Montagu's boatman' although he was in effect the harbour master and he lived in the Master Builder's House at Bucklers Hard. Captain Widnell described him as being 'in his sixties, silent, bearded'.

John was introducing Pearl to the people and landscapes that made up his world, a world that she embraced with enthusiasm. In effect, Pearl jumped a generation when she married John – he was more than twice her age – and she adjusted her interests to reflect those of her husband, interests which were firmly grounded in the life of the Beaulieu Estate. The world of London society receded and the dancing virtually stopped. She never wrote of John as she had of Harry that it was 'too lovely' dancing with him only noting rather sadly on 19 May 1924 after going to two dances alone – *John does hate dances so.*

John Montagu was a complex character, a highly intelligent and intellectually curious man who could not bear to be trammelled. More than 30 years earlier, an Oxford contemporary at New College had observed him as 'too restless a spirit to fit into the ordinary life of a college.' By the time he married Pearl, both the need for intellectual stimulus and action and the broad scope of his activities were long established. The settled state of marriage could not modify his behaviour; on the contrary the presence of a partner able to undertake the responsibility of household organisation and to help entertain the many guests who found their way to Beaulieu, relieved him of a burden and provided an emotional stability that gave him greater freedom for his many pursuits. He never embraced the vogue for cocktail parties that were so much a feature of twenties' society, and which would have been meat and drink to Pearl.

'Our first spree!!'

Within a few days of their marriage John had resumed the familiar pattern of his life balancing his business and professional life in London with friends and sporting interests at Beaulieu and beyond, as Pearl recorded. The presence of his young wife did not cause him to slow down –

> *John and I had 8.30 breakfast in his Study and at 8.55 Teddie motored us and Jane into Southampton West and we caught the 9.40 from there. We have got a hired Beardmore car for the two days we are up – so I dropped John and Jane at his office then went home to South Street, then went to lunch with Gladys and Cyril, so nice seeing them – took*

Gladys in the car shopping till 3.30 and went to fetch John at 3.45. He and I shopped, then teaed at the RAC, then at 5.30 he and I went back to South Street where we are staying 2 nights (Mum is away). He and I dined at the Ritz at 7 – the first time we have ever dined out alone!! Great fun. A pouring wet evening – luckily we had the car. We went on to 'At the Villa Rose' at the Strand Theatre – too excellent and very exciting .... Loved our evening together – our first spree!! (18 AUGUST)

Went straight to Waterloo and came down by the 2.30 .... John and I got out at Southampton West where Teddie met us with the Delage – we went straight to Andrew's works to see the new Rolls (Royce) and how the body was getting on. They really promise it to us by Monday 31st but there is a lot of work on her – she is going to be lovely and very comfy .... A gorgeous evening – we sat about and walked in the garden till 7.30 – Very happy to be in our beautiful and peaceful home again. (20 AUGUST)

In the weeks at Beaulieu following her marriage, Pearl began to explore her new home with John meanwhile recording her impressions of people and places –

Rained between 7 and 9 but dull and fine after .... At 4 Tommie Troubridge, John and I motored to Warren Farm where we found Mr Le Marchant and the keepers waiting for us – we walked on to Blackwater, which was an old salt pan of 17th and 18th centuries, there were a lot duck and teal there, including mallard, teal, garganey (one was shot, very rare), shovellers, coot, water hens, moor hen, dab chick, snipe. (23 AUGUST)

By the end of August, the shape of Pearl's future life was being established with its network of relationships and the routine of visiting and entertaining –

A gorgeous day again and quite hot – able to wear summer dress again. At 12.50 we motored over to The House on the Shore to lunch with Mrs Du Cane [then the tenant] *.... We had a very nice lunch then Mrs Du Cane showed me over the house; it is really too charming – John took huge pains when he built it – all oak, 432 oaks in it, mostly John's furniture – a lot of which I covet!! A perfect day .... John caught a 2 lb sea trout.*
(25 AUGUST)

John had taken great care in the construction of the house known as the House on the Shore which was let to a tenant when he married Pearl. He and Pearl decamped there in October 1922 for two months while Palace House was let to the film producer and director J. Stuart Blackton for the making of his film *The Virgin Queen*.

Another lovely day. Spent a hectic morning seeing to flowers, writing tables, Mummy's room etc. for it all to be nice when she comes tonight …. Mum is delighted with Palace House and all our wedding presents out. At 8 Sir T and Louise and Rosemary Troubridge, Lady Pinckney, Col Goodenough and George Farrar dined. We were 10 — our first dinner party — it went off very well. (27 AUGUST)

The following day John and Pearl gave a garden party for the tenants and the village to celebrate their marriage —

Rested after lunch and at 4 all the tenants and village people began to arrive and the band played on the lawn. Tents for tea and an entertainment went on the East Lawn and we all helped them, about 400 to tea, which was all organised by the dear Vicar and Miss Jane Burden. Then later, on the West Lawn, by the sun dial, Mr Powell made a short speech and handed John the list of names of all the subscribers on the Manor of a cheque as wedding present to John, with which John is to buy a set of book cases. (28 AUGUST)

John's speech of thanks reflected both his commitment to Beaulieu as well as his future hopes —

I have never felt your kindness for me more warmly than on this occasion, when I have the honour and pleasure of presenting my bride to you. I hope she will make herself thoroughly at home in Beaulieu, and I feel sure you will help her to do so …. I want you to feel that we shall together endeavour to carry on the traditions of the Manor and before very long I hope Lady Montagu will know you all not only by sight, but personally and by name. She is very glad to make your acquaintance today, and hopes to keep always in close touch with you. I know you will always give her a warm welcome.

There were certain defined responsibilities that Pearl was expected to undertake and running Palace House efficiently was one of them. Her achievement in making a home there was warmly acknowledged by John, as a letter written by him on 2 October 1923, when Pearl was in the final stages of pregnancy, reveals —

I often think that present comfort (what a bad pen!) obscures my sense of what I owe to the maker of that comfort. When I think of my home today welcoming, homely and gracious and what it was in former years I yearn towards the maker of that change.

Pearl also took on the role of stepmother to John's younger daughter, Elizabeth, who had been born in 1909, 20 years after the birth of his eldest daughter, Helen. At this point Helen was living in the United States. Chronologically, Pearl was sandwiched between the two, five years younger than Helen and 14 years older than Elizabeth. Like Pearl, Elizabeth was lively, and enjoyed sports and being active. There it seemed the similarity ended. The enduring link between them was John. Elizabeth was very much her father's daughter in her cast of mind and robust personality with the same distaste for what she called *society rigmarole*. She possessed both intellectual curiosity and creative originality that took no regard of the conventions of the day, two attributes which were the hallmarks of John's character.

Pearl's upbringing had been framed for the most part by the female members of her family – her mother, the firm-minded Aunt Vi, her half-sisters, her young cousin Beryl, her sister Gladys in particular – these were close and companionate relationships. There was a notable lack of men and boys in her immediate family circle and the death of her father rendered the nuclear household an all-feminine one. In particular she regarded her mother with a mixture of deference and devotion and, aware that her marriage effectively left her mother alone in London, did all she could to include Clara in her new life.

Pearl willingly and conscientiously undertook responsibility for the details of Elizabeth's welfare with the result that the child was soon enfolded into her new life –

> *Elizabeth came up from her school .... we first went to see about her riding clothes, then we were to see Parkie* [the surgeon Sir Thomas Parkinson] *at 12. John joined me there, then took her to Mr Rose the dentist at 12.30, there had a been a muddle so he didn't expect her, so he couldn't do much and says she must come back tomorrow. Went back to the office and we had to decide to keep her up over tomorrow. Eliz hugely pleased!! .... Then I took Eliz to the new Gallery cinema – got back to John's office at 6!! We are putting her up at South Street for tonight.* (26 OCTOBER)

Elizabeth had been despatched to a boarding school at Hindhead during her mother's last illness in 1919. It was not a happy experience. Elizabeth later described the conditions there –

> *...no modern sanitation ... in many ways Dickensian ... three earth closets among thirty girls, no heating, and some indifferent teachers.*

After a visit there, Pearl realised that a change was essential. The result was that Elizabeth was rescued speedily from this environment and sent to a far better school at Eastbourne. The move was judged to be a success as Pearl reported when she and John made their first visit there –

> *Eliz looking so well and happy. J delighted with school.* (24 MARCH 1921)

'So happy here with my John'

While John had the opportunity to pursue his activities and to select his friends and companions before and after the wedding, it was not so for Pearl constrained as she was by the expectations and demands that applied to women in her position. The world in which she was raised expected her to stick to the rules and not challenge them. She could not afford to dispense with the conventions in the way that John did on occasion, but both Pearl and John were very similar in their huge energy and sociability and their liking for new experiences.

Marriage to John gave Pearl a rich life experience as well as the opportunity to demonstrate her intelligence and competence in a much larger sphere, qualities which John recognised and prized as he wrote to her in June 1928 –

> *Your pluck and cool sense always come to the front when crises occur domestic and otherwise.*

What is apparent from even the earliest days of marriage is how busy Pearl was. If she ever wanted to reflect on the speed with which her life had changed and the personality of the man she had married, there was hardly any time to do so. John's passion for the river – he was a dedicated fisherman, for his motorboat, for shooting, for life on the estate and for seeing his friends now included Pearl, but nevertheless he maintained his usual relentless pace.

Throughout their married life, John continued his habit of commuting between London and Beaulieu, often going to London for day. His base in London was his office at 62 Pall Mall where he worked with his secretary, Jane Clowes. A professional journalist, he had founded and edited *The Car Illustrated* until he joined the army in 1914, although he continued to write for both the motoring and national press. He was also an active member of the House of Lords.

Pearl with her mother and the young Elizabeth Montagu. Pearl described her future stepdaughter as a *perfect darling, red hair, blue eyes and a beautiful complexion* when she first met Elizabeth in July 1920.

Pearl's honeymoon journey with John was a motoring holiday to France with their new Rolls-Royce Phantom I. The car had been purpose built for John and it was judged a great success with Pearl noting that *She really is wonderful, she goes up all hills at 50 miles per hour and then only half the throttle, and so silent.*

Political, motoring, aeronautical and social interests required his frequent presence at meetings and dinners in London. How aware Pearl was of these different activities when they married, and the extent to which claimed him, is unclear. But she had begun to get a sense of John as a public figure when she read a comment in the press when their engagement was announced –

> *The Ladies Pictorial says Lord Montagu is one of the men who matter which pleased me very much.* (30 JUNE 1920)

Quite apart from running the Beaulieu Estate, John also had business interests in Lancashire inherited from his father (see page 168). He was active in local politics, particularly in the administration of the New Forest. In addition, he was a long-time member of the Hampshire County Council, a large administrative area then including part of present-day Dorset.

At the beginning of September, John and Pearl left Beaulieu for France, the first of many overseas trips they made, but not until Pearl had seen John discharging yet another responsibility –

> *I went with John to the Hythe Bench at 10 – most interesting and amusing to see John and 4 other JPs* [Justices of the Peace] *dispensing justice indifferently …. After dinner, at 9.45 John and I and Speake motored into Southampton docks in the Ford, as the new Rolls went ahead with Teddie. So interesting, seeing the Rolls embarked by the big crane as she weighed 38 cwt, all loaded. We sailed at 12.15 in the Hantonia, the same ship which brought John back after the Persia!* [John had been on his way to India in December 1915 when the ship was torpedoed by a German U-boat.] *Had two beautiful saloon cabins and a wonderful night – very calm.* (3 SEPTEMBER 1920)

Their journey – *the first trip in our beautiful new Rolls* – was to the spa town of Bagnoles-de-l'Orne in Normandy which was becoming popular with overseas visitors. The waters there were thought to be beneficial for rheumatic, circulatory and gynaecological disorders – Pearl and John both took the cure, Pearl to treat veins in her legs. Significantly, she noted –

> *So happy here with my John – quite alone really more so than at Beaulieu.* (6 SEPTEMBER)

'A very charming cheery party'

On their return Pearl had to have another operation – this time a dilation and curettage – a procedure often performed after miscarriage. Whatever the reason for this, there was a prolonged stay in London while she recovered noting on 3 October, *Feeling very well, so maddening having to lie in bed when there is so much to do at Beaulieu.* But there were compensations and the opportunity to see something of the extremely wide scope of John's interests –

> *Stayed in the sitting room and wrote all morning till John came back from his office at 1.15 and he and I had lunch together – then he went off to a Board, and I joined him in a taxi at 3 and then we went off the Guildhall together to the Air conference. I sat up in the gallery and heard too beautifully Sir Trevor Dawson on air ships …. John moved the Resolution that there should be an Annual Air Conference and Sir T Dawson seconded it and it was unanimously carried.* (14 OCTOBER)

The three-day Air Conference had been called to discuss the fledgling aviation industry and its future commercial and military development. Those present included Winston Churchill, then Secretary of State for War and Secretary of State for Air, and Hugh Trenchard, the first Chief of the Air Staff recently reappointed by Churchill. Sir Trevor Dawson was managing director of the armaments manufacturer, Vickers.

Whether in town or at home, Pearl was fully occupied in the early months of her marriage. Even she occasionally found the pace too demanding –

> *Sonia and Rolie's wedding.* [Roland was the Cubitt's eldest surviving son] *John and I had lunch at 1 and then we went to the Guards Chapel …. The Bishop of Winchester never turned up and at the last minute Canon Chichester married them …. We then went on to 16 Grosvenor Street – a dense crowd. John didn't stay long ….Rolie and Sonia looking so happy, wonderful presents and her jewels marvellous. …. John and I dined at 7 with the Andersons ….Very tired.* (16 NOVEMBER 1920)

> *I stayed in bed till lunch as was so tired. Had 12.45 lunch and then Mum fetched me in a Brougham at 1.10 and we went to Henry VII chapel at Westminster Abbey for Patience Basset and Victor Agar Robartes wedding at 2 ….Went and had my hair waved at Emiles, and then Mum dropped me at 62 Pall Mall, and we went back and had a rest. Then at 7.30 we went to the big Aeronautical Society Dinner in the Connaught Rooms – 122 people altogether …. Dashed back to the hotel and changed my dress into my wedding dress … put my tiara on for the first time. John had all his decorations and orders and we got to Chelsea House at 10.40. The dance for the King and Queen of Spain and the coming out of the Dona Philippa. Everyone looked very well in tiaras and decorations. Saw such a lot of people we knew. John and I had supper together and several dances and then we went back at 1.* (17 NOVEMBER 1920)

Through John, Pearl's had the opportunity to widen her own circle considerably, something that greatly appealed to her social instincts. She and John began to make overnight visits to friends and one such visit was to the home of the industrialist, Sir Alfred Mond, and his wife –

In November 1920, Pearl and John went to a dance in London for the King and Queen of Spain, one of the very rare occasions when John could be persuaded on to a dance floor. Pearl's love of society life is evident in her diary. Before her marriage she often notes that she 'shopped hard, danced hard' and never fails to record the names of people at events.

Melchet Park, Romsey
We left Beaulieu at 9.30 and motored over to the Melchet Park, the Monds …. Such
a lovely house and gorgeous things in it. My room is all old painted Venetian Oriental
furniture. A very charming cheery party. Everything marvellously done. (20 NOVEMBER)

The celebrations that first Christmas at Beaulieu in 1920 included a fancy dress dance for family
and friends in the Domus, originally the lay brothers' dormitory of the old Cistercian Abbey –

Mummy, Gladys, Cyril and I lunched with Mr Le Marchant at Little Marsh. Tommie,
Laura and Rosemary left us by the 2.15 to make room for the rest of our party …. We
all had a good rest before dinner and then dressed up in Fancy Dresses. John was 'John
Duke of Montagu', in brown cloth suit of clothes and white wig, and I hired a flowered
silk Georgian dress with powdered wig. Gladys hired a lovely blue silk dress of Romney
times with wig. Mum had a wig, Lena Agar as Rosalinde, Violet Seely as a rainbow!
Cyril in Charles I suit. Archie Cubitt and Mr Bremner didn't arrive till after 8 instead
of 7.15 as their engine broke down so they hurriedly dressed …. Such a pretty sight,
fancy dress in the old room. It was run very well by the Beaulieu Dance Club and only
130 people so was not overcrowded …. Mummy, Gladys, Cyril, John and I came home
at 1 but the others stayed till 3.15. It was a great success. Lady Mond brought over a
party. (29 DECEMBER)

But there were occasions in the early days when, in John's absence, Pearl felt isolated on her own
in the then remote location of Beaulieu, noting on one occasion –

Wonderful to have him back again. Very lonely without him. (25 NOVEMBER 1920)

The diary also suggests that Pearl would have welcomed a great deal more privacy with John.
After one holiday in 1925 she wrote –

It has been a blissful three weeks – quite alone with my darling John – for the first time
really since our first honeymoon in August and September 1920. (27 JUNE)

The focus of Pearl's life changed radically after her marriage with her interests thenceforth reflecting primarily those of
her husband. John was a keen sailor taking every opportunity to be out on the Beaulieu River and the Solent. Pearl came
to share his enthusiasm and they spent many hours on John's motorboat *Cygnet*.

But John's instincts about Pearl had been right. As he had hoped, the affection and love between them both strengthened and deepened over the years. In a letter to John, after one of their few times of quiet together, Pearl wrote –

My very own, never to be forgotten was our wondrous few days together, my love – I shall always remember it … (MAY 1928)

Nurse Barrett went off at 9.20 for her 3 weeks holiday. Greatly relieved to find Anne is quite happy with Nurse Moore. Went off to sleep alright – no tears. This afternoon we took Anne for a drive & Eliz: & Bunny in the car. Anne went to bed quite contented with new Nannie.

John went up by the 9.57. Eliz: went to see her father off at Brockenhurst. I stayed in bed to day. At 3.15 Nurse Moore Anne, Miss Knott & Eliz! went off to Fawley to spend the afternoon with the Cokes. Eliz: went & fished

The most devine day — so hot & sunny. after having had 11 inchs of rain since Feb: 15th — it is about time it stopped. Stayed in bed again today.

6
THE NURSERY PARTY

mummy who should have arrived at 8. from Sthampton where Ted went to meet her at 7. a.m. did not arrive till 8.55 as the boat was an hour late. She left Belagio on Lake Como on monday. She is looking so well having been away 3 months abroad including Rome & Florence. Elizabeth & Phyllis Knott went out at 1.25 & miss

CHAPTER 6

THE NURSERY PARTY

On 1 January 1921, Pearl summed up her feelings about the first months of her married life –

> *John and I are very very happy, too wonderful and perhaps this time next year we shall have a little baby, only so praying it may be a son and heir.*

The birth of a boy was of great importance to the hopes of both John and Pearl for the future. At that point John's heir was his younger daughter, Elizabeth; he had disinherited his elder daughter, Helen, when she had defied him to pursue a career on the stage.

Clara stayed with Pearl for most of January that year, accompanying her daughter on visits around the neighbourhood while John was away in London or out shooting with friends –

> *A nice morning early, and John went off by the 8.5 to London for the day. It started to deluge at 12 but stopped about lunch time …. Mum and I went out in the car Hythe way and called on various people.* (12 JANUARY)

By mid-January Pearl was under orders from her doctor to take things quietly – the first hint that she was expecting a child. Her interpretation of a quiet life may well have differed from the medical version: the next few weeks seem to have been especially busy with a round of engagements in Hampshire and London, and two motoring trips away with John. Even when instructed to rest in bed, Pearl made the best use of time by catching up on other tasks –

> *A hurricane in the night and blowing and raining still – with moments of sunshine. In bed again all day. Made jewellery lists with Speake and then the rest of the day I did accounts, 4 different ones till my head reeled.* (18 JANUARY)

John and Pearl were reunited with Anne, their eldest daughter, in April 1922 on their return from their four-month trip to India. Characteristically, although Pearl doesn't record missing Anne whilst she was away – and indeed hardly mentions her – the diary entry of 16 April reveals her feelings, *I am so thrilled at the thought of seeing her tomorrow.*

It was not until the beginning of February, that Pearl made the first direct mention of her pregnancy when she was able to catch up with an old friend in London –

Speake came with me in the car, went to the Regina where Mum met me, then chose some stuff at Lewis – then I lunched with Melita Hely-Hutchinson in the little house, 14 Chester Terrace, they have just taken. We haven't seen each other since our weddings on the 10th and 11th of August, and are now both expecting infants, she in May and I in August!! (2 FEBRUARY)

Life continued at its usual hectic pace but by the middle of May even Pearl was forced to admit that there were limits to her stamina –

Didn't sleep very well and feel thoroughly overtired, so stayed in bed all today. Very annoying how little I can do without getting tired now – I suppose I stood too long last evening. (15 MAY)

June and July were hot and dry months with occasional downpours of rain. Although Pearl enjoyed the fine days and evenings at Beaulieu, the heat was oppressive –

As hot as ever – the heat was so awful one couldn't sleep. (12 JULY)

Increasingly, Pearl was preoccupied by hopes for a son, although the day before she was due to go to London for the birth, 11-year-old Elizabeth provided something of a distraction –

Went to church this morning, everyone so nice to me after and wished me the best of luck! How little does one know what the future will bring forth – and how we pray for a little son. We had tea at 4.30, then Tommie, Mummy and Joan Woodroffe, John and I went for a slow drive round by North Gate, Hythe, Dibden and home by Hill Top which was so nice. Elizabeth didn't want to come! She has been in a very rampageous and tiresome mood today. (21 AUGUST)

Once Pearl was settled in London at Clara's house in South Street, the final preparations for the baby's arrival were put in place. As was usual for middle-class women in the 1920s, Pearl's baby would be born at home, in her mother's house, and not in a maternity hospital –

*At 11.30 Mummy, Gladys and I went out in a Victoria and did shoppings till 1.30 ....
I rested after lunch – fearful thunderstorm at 4 – never heard worse thunder and torrents
of rain. My nurse, Nurse Spencer, arrived at 4.30 – so now she has come and we are
installed here. I hope my little one will not keep me waiting long ...* (23 AUGUST)

But Pearl had nearly six weeks to wait. She kept busy seeing friends and family, with John
staying in Thurloe Square when he was in London. Clara arranged outings and theatre visits to
divert her, and Pearl also managed to do some shopping for an extended trip to India that she
and John had been planning since June, but nevertheless the weeks dragged on –

Very hot. Nurse, Mummy and I walked to Harrods and we saw about prams, E's
[Elizabeth's] *clothes etc. I am very energetic and walk every morning for 2 hours and
hope that will hurry JJ* [John Junior] *up!!* (8 SEPTEMBER)

*We shopped till lunch. This afternoon Mummy took me to 'Woman to Woman' at the
Royalty, an excellent new play ... they all acted wonderfully well and it was the most
attractive and pathetic play – everyone sobbed and we came away with very red eyes – but
thoroughly enjoyed it.* (10 SEPTEMBER)

*I came down and had breakfast with John – Dr Barncroft came to see me – he says
things are decidedly further on but still JJ seems very bashful – too annoying – he is 15
days late!! I walked hard all the morning.* (14 SEPTEMBER)

Away in Beaulieu, John was feeling the absence of Pearl. On 16 September he wrote –

*My beloved woman. Such a wonderful autumn morning here with a touch of frost early.
I and we all do wish you were here to enjoy it. For myself I don't enjoy this now you
are away, like I do when you are here. They haven't the same zest in them at all ....*

*Everyone here is agog about you but I tell them all is well and 'wait and see'. J.J. knows
best and he is growing and developing all the time with his Mummy's help and will hop
out beautifully made one day soon .... My own beloved my heart is always with you,
and I'm thinking about you consciously or unconsciously all the time. Keep well and be
careful of yourself.*

A week later, things were still no further forward. Pearl's solution was yet more shopping and another trip to the theatre –

Stuffy and hot. Dr Bancroft came again. JJ seems no nearer arriving! Mum and I shopped in Harrods till lunch at 1. At 2.15 we went off to 'The Adventures of Ambrose Applejohn', Hackett's new play at the Criterion, an excellent farce and killingly funny from beginning to end – it was packed with people. (24 SEPTEMBER)

'Better luck next time'

It was not until very early on Tuesday 4 October, after a 21-hour labour, that the founder member of what Pearl was later to call the 'nursery party' finally arrived –

One of the first photographs of Anne Montagu at just over three weeks old, taken at a photographer's studio in London on 28 October 1921, the day before Pearl brought her home to Beaulieu. It was a struggle to get the pictures as Pearl recorded in her diary that day – *Poor little girl had not slept all the morning and was howling when we got there. We had an awful job to get any photos but with the aid of sugar and water we hope for the best!*

Woke up at 3 a.m. [on Monday 3 October] *feeling unwell pains. Sat up and read, as pains increased. Nurse very excited as baby had begun after five weeks. Got up after breakfast and went down into clean room where I alternately read, worked or walked about – sent John a wire. Pains much worse by lunch time so ate no lunch. Was sick, pains worse and continued. Dr Bancroft looked in once or twice. John arrived 5.15 – only just saw him. Sent for Bancroft who came at 6.30 when I went to bed. Remained with me all the time till 12.30 when baby was born. Gave me chloroform all the time but not sufficient to be unconscious.*

It was a very long affair as none of the pains would now do their work. JJ turned out to be a daughter which is very sad – but better luck next time and she is a darling.

The baby was named Anne Rachel Pearl. If John felt disappointment at the arrival of another daughter – his fourth, including his natural child by his former secretary, Eleanor Thornton – he did not express it to Pearl. A letter written by him on 7 October shows his overwhelming concern for Pearl's health and his fear of losing her. This fear was not groundless – one in 20 women did not survive childbirth in the early 1920s –

Thank God you are through the danger of childbirth. I had a haunting dread ever since I got that telegram that something might have happen to you, and that all my life, my hope, and our wonderful love might crash down. Those hours seemed endless to me, as they must have to you, my sweet wonderful wife.

From the first, the baby thrived –

Little Anne is a week old today and wonderful thing has put on 1 oz in the week and they generally either lose or remain the same for first week so it shows how strong and well she is. (11 OCTOBER)

Pearl luxuriated in the comfort of her mother's house until the time came to return to Beaulieu –

My John arrived here at 1.14 – came up from Beaulieu and now on Saturday we are going back to Beaulieu together, on Saturday morning I shall have been away for 9 weeks since August 22nd, with darling little Ma. It has been so comfy and lovely being here.

Three weeks today since Anne was born, she was weighed today and has put on 6 oz, so has put on 21 oz in 21 days. (25 OCTOBER)

Very excited – going home today. At 12 Mummy, Nurse, little Anne and I left South Street on a taxi for Waterloo, Anne wide awake and so good! John met us .... We had a very comfortable journey and lunch in the carriage. Anne only cried before her bottle. We arrived at Brockenhurst at 2.29 where Mr Leslie Scott kindly sent his closed car to meet us. A gorgeous day and perfect evening, so warm and no wind .... So lovely to be home again. (29 OCTOBER)

Nurse Barrett arrived on 5 November to take over the responsibility for Anne, replacing Nurse Spencer who had been employed as a maternity nurse for the period immediately before and after the baby's arrival –

Nurse Barrett came today. She seems so nice and Nurse Spencer is so taken with her – she was 10 years with Margaret Buccleuch, so nice to have been someone who has been in the family.

Nurse Barrett became an important part of household at Palace House. The nursery came under her control and she had complete responsibility for Anne's welfare. Pearl, like most women in her position, was expected to leave the main care of her child to someone else. This ensured that she had time to continue her estate and public duties. The result was that the day-to-day experience of motherhood was to be at one remove.

Despite this, the diary shows how much pleasure Pearl took in her daughter. According to the convention of the day, Pearl either visited the nursery or had Anne downstairs at certain fixed times. Occasionally the timing went awry – *Got back late, so couldn't have baby Anne downstairs* (30 APRIL 1922) – but this was very much the exception with Pearl relishing the time spent with Anne – *Anne came down at 5.30 and we 'baby worshipped' till 6.20* (2 MAY 1922). When in the summer of 1922 Anne and her nurse went to stay at Denbies with the Ashcombes in advance of Pearl's visit there with John, Pearl lamented on returning to Beaulieu –

John's anxiety for Pearl's safety in childbirth and his relief that both she and their daughter survived is evident in a letter he wrote to Pearl just after Anne was born – *I have you still, and our babe, us three now, another rivet in the chain of love* (7 October 1921).

John and I went home by the 4.30. Missed Anne so much when we arrived back to find an empty nursery. (29 JUNE)

When Anne was two months old John and Pearl left on an extended visit to India and there was virtually no mention of Anne in Pearl's diary until her return to Beaulieu –

Home sweet home again after 4 months abroad. So thrilled at seeing the wee Anne again – who is now aged 6¼ months and she was only 11 weeks when we left…. I dashed into the inner hall and found our wee Anne looking too divine in Barrett's arms, sitting

up and holding out her little hands. She was so friendly to us both — as if she had known us always — she has a very little fairish red hair, and the prettiest little features!
(17 APRIL 1922)

The structure of Pearl's life meant that she was frequently separated from her daughter. In Anne's first year, Pearl was away from home for nearly five months, discounting London visits.

'Little flower of our love'

Pearl documented only her first pregnancy in detail. In early 1923, she spent nearly two months in the south of France with John. On 20 March she was reunited with the 17-month-old Anne who *made great friends with me almost at once.*

By now Pearl was pregnant with her second child. She hints at this with references to feeling tired and a visit from the local doctor on 28 April — *Dr Maturin came to see me at 6.15. I stayed in bed for dinner* — but is otherwise silent until the arrival of the maternity nurse at Beaulieu on 13 October *…now I can have my baby anytime, the sooner the better!!* John referred to the coming child as *the next little flower of our love* assuring Pearl in a letter *do remember that if it is boy or girl it matters not.*

Pearl's description of the birth was succinct —

Woke up at 12.50 a.m. with first pains, went and called Nurse, discussed matters and decided I had started my baby, as they came very much nearer together and stronger than they did with Anne …. Waters broke, pain so Nurse decided to telephone for Dr Maturin who was here with us within half hour. Pains got very bad and I was given chloroform at once. 5.30 It was all over very quickly. I came round about 6.45. Dr M told me that it was the wrong sex which did not surprise me and also that it was not born alive.

I was very dazed so did not take much in. I could not get over how very much quicker it was than with Anne. From start to finish it was only 5½ hours, instead of 22 hours. Later on I asked Dr Maturin to come and explain what had happened. He was so nice and told me what had happened. It was a complicated breech which meant that the baby came tail first instead of head first, which means that it was strangled by the cord. Nurse told me after that the baby was a little bigger than Anne and its hair was darker than hers and more of it.

I forgot to say that as soon I started having the pains I went into John's room. I am going to stay here for the whole time as there is a single bed, a coal fire and easier to keep warm. (8 NOVEMBER)

There is no indication that Pearl even saw her second child. She seems to have felt very differently about this pregnancy, and was understandably cautious about expressing her hopes for a son. Why she decided to remain in Beaulieu rather than go to London is not clear. Whatever her emotions she was outwardly buoyant –

Slept the whole night through …. Poor Mummy and John did not sleep well so I teased them, said the patient was behaving better than the parents … (9 NOVEMBER)

and appreciative of all that was done to cheer her up –

Gladys and Cyril sent me a most lovely little bottle of Coty's concentrated bouquet scent, a lovely box of red and pink carnations from Mrs Bolton, also a box of sweets, chocolate Tunbridge Wells wafers, honey cakes from Lady Swaythling …. My room is a perfect bower of flowers. (15 NOVEMBER)

It is only in her final diary entry for 1923 that she revealed something of her underlying feelings –

The last day of the old year – it has been a dreary one for me – from January to November expecting my baby and then that it should have been born dead! It will have been a whole year before I feel myself again!

Characteristically, Pearl did not dwell on her loss in her diary. It was only years later on hearing the news that her cousin Tom and his wife Nancy had lost their daughter in childbirth that she expressed something of the deep sense of bereavement she had gone through 14 years earlier with the death of this second child –

Beryl rang up at 8.30 and told me the tragic news that they could not save Nancy and Tom's little baby girl after the Caesarean operation at 9 pm they found her strangled by the cord! A perfect little baby as mine was which I lost in 1922. It is just so tragic – Nancy had set her heart on this wee babe and given herself up so completely to it!

And then for this tragedy to happen! Nancy is alright so far but she must have 3 or 4 fearful days of pain followed by the misery and utter forlornness which follows losing one's babe. (14 JULY 1937)

'The most amusing and wonderful clothes'

In May 1924 Nurse Barrett left. Her departure was a big loss for both Pearl and Anne –

Dear Nannie Barrett went off this morning. She has been with Anne ever since the month [after the birth] *and I can't bear her going, just 2½ years. She wants to find a place in Scotland or North of England and London as she always feels so ill at Beaulieu. Anne was quite good all day but it was when she was being put to bed she began to cry. It is a big break in her little life.* (12 MAY)

Nannie Champ took over the nursery. Anne was now an energetic toddler, developing a will of her own –

Had a very exhausting morning with Anne who was very naughty. I had two real fights with her. She wouldn't sleep this morning so for a punishment we didn't take her in the car to Lymington and she was put to bed after lunch. (30 JULY)

By August 1924 Pearl was pregnant once more. She was to have five pregnancies in less than seven years in a decade when curves were unfashionable – everything was straight lines, with short, tubular dresses topped by small, bell-shaped hats. For the fashion-loving Pearl, this must have been particularly galling as she noted after seeing the new season's creations –

… most amusing and wonderful clothes, all skin tight – so not much good for me this winter. (23 SEPTEMBER)

This baby was born at Clara's house in London, and caught everyone unawares –

Woke up at 6.30 a.m. with three or four pains so woke John and we telephoned and told

Caroline Montagu was born on 13 February 1925. Pearl and John's third daughter (their second child had been stillborn), was baptised in the Abbey Church in Beaulieu in April that year, Pearl noting – *Caroline wore the same christening robe Eliz and Anne wore, and a new christening cloak on which we put old lace, and then she had a lovely old Brussels lace veil, right over her and a bonnet Grannie gave her.* Pearl's cousin, Beryl Dugdale, was one of the godparents.

Dr Bott. Then got straight on to Nurse Spencer at Forest Row. Most luxurious having a telephone in one's bedroom .... Lucky Nurse Spencer was able to catch the 8.30 train so got here quite early ....The baby arrived and I was told it was another girl. (13 FEBRUARY)

A very neat little baby of 8lbs 4ozs ... It seems I failed that I should not have produced a son yet. I have felt so different all along this baby, it coming early instead of late lulled me to think it really was a boy this time ....We think we are going to call her Caroline. (14 FEBRUARY)

However Pearl's sense of failure was not shared by the outwardly pragmatic John who wrote to her on the night of Caroline's birth –

I must write you a v short letter to greet you if you wake before I call in the morning. So long as you are safe and recovering from the strain and pain of childbirth I care not what sex your darling baby may be and its yours and mine, sweet woman, just the same. Keep calm, get well, and we'll have a wonderful time together when you are well again. I felt for you so much today and yet I couldn't do anything to help.

Anne was introduced to her sister –

Anne saw Caroline for first time when Spencer brought her in from walk. Anne was very awe inspired, went very pink and held Granny's hand very tight and said nothing I think she must have thought it would be bigger, as she has never seen a tiny baby before! (19 MARCH)

'Quite dazed'

The year 1926 proved to be a memorable, both nationally and for Pearl and John. The industrial unrest that had been simmering for years was threatening to become a reality, fuelling fears of revolution. The immediate focus was the hardship experienced by Britain's mineworkers who were facing the prospect of increased hours and decreased wages. Pearl was distanced from the industrial epicentre, literally and metaphorically, but was nevertheless very aware of events –

The Colliers stopped work today – as all negotiations broke down last night after an all day sitting of the various Trade Unions and the Cabinet meetings. After 9 months of hard work .... All to no avail. (3 MAY)

A 1925 snapshot of Pearl, Anne and Caroline at Beaulieu.

She was pregnant once more but remained silent until the pregnancy was well advanced –

> *Our Wedding Day 6 years ago, 6 blissfully happy years and now we have Anne aged 4 years 10 months, and Caroline 1½ years and another little feller coming in October who we hope is a little boy.* (10 AUGUST)

At the beginning of October Pearl again made the now-familiar journey to London for the birth at Clara's house. The labour began after a busy day shopping –

Mummy and I went out shopping and then to our flat to see about new loose covers. Beryl and John lunched then he and I shopped together. Uncle Dick and Islay and Rachel Forster came to tea. Islay stayed till 7.20 by which time I felt sure I had my first pain – warned Nurse Spencer and went down to dinner which Aunt Vi came to. Had 4 pains at dinner so while I, Aunt Vi and Mummy were in the drawing room, Nurse Spencer and maids got everything ready …. we sent for Dr Bott at 3.30 a.m. (19 OCTOBER)

Overjoyed to hear it was a boy! He was born at 5.45 a.m. at his grannie's house, 29 South Street, Thurloe Square. Brought into the world by Dr Bott, Nurse Spencer. John who was sleeping at our flat, came round and was here in time. Oh!! The excitement hit. John was quite stunned, hardly took it in. He weighed exactly 8 lbs and a neat little fellow like Anne was …. The news was in the first edition of the evening papers …. I had lots of wires. John came in to see me at 5 o'clock for a little bit and said Reuters is broadcasting the news at 7 and 10 p.m. (20 OCTOBER)

Slept very well all the night and the little John gave Nurse Spencer a very good night too, so every body smiling. John came round to see me before lunch. He was snowed under with letters at 62. Telegrams pouring in here in packets of 10. I am beginning to realise I have a little boy but John is quite dazed. It is such a complete change to his whole life as he said today, he will have to alter his will and many deeds, as he has suddenly got an heir. (21 OCTOBER)

Pearl and John differed in their preference for names but there was a pressing reason for resolving the question without delay. In the event, John's choice prevailed –

I want him to be called John Henry Barrington. John wants him to be Edward John Barrington. They are going to discuss it at Beaulieu this weekend and we have got to finally settle on Monday as Debrett must have it for this year's publication on Tuesday. (21 OCTOBER)

John holding the four-week-old Edward on the day he was christened. He marked the baby's birth by making a special gift to Pearl as she recorded on 29 October – *On his way here he went to Hemings the jewellers, the darling has settled to quite spoil me, by giving me the emerald and diamond heart ring as well as the diamond bandeau. And Hemings is making the centre of it into a brooch and the two end sprays into earrings. The little emerald and diamond ring, I shall wear it, I simply love it and he is going to have an inscription put in the ring – Our boy Oct 20th 1926.*

The birth of a boy on 20 October 1926 was far more than a private event. It not only changed the dynamic of family life fundamentally but had big implications for the future of Beaulieu and everyone who lived there. Elizabeth was no longer the heir to the estate, a change of role that she welcomed. There was now a son to inherit both the land and the title. The succession was secure.

Anne and Caroline were introduced to their brother –

> *Anne asked her daddy where we got the little boy from and he said that is Mummy's secret!! She will tell you!!* (23 OCTOBER)

> *Caroline was so sweet and called him the little bébé and said hush! hush!* (31 OCTOBER)

Four weeks later, the baby was christened in Beaulieu Church –

> *Little EDWARD JOHN BARRINGTON's christening day. Glorious early but clouded over at 12 and we were very fearful as to the rain keeping off …. At 2.55 John and I, Nurse Champ holding baby and Nurse Spencer walked over to church – the press photographers turned up in force!! The church was absolutely packed – all ticket holders and the font most beautifully decorated by Miss Cheshire, white Madonna lilies, white chrysanthemums, smilax and white heather …. Dear Daddy Powles* [the vicar of Beaulieu] *took the service so beautifully and little Edward was so good – he didn't cry at all and just grunted when it was all over.* (28 NOVEMBER)

There is a sense that Edward's arrival had shaken both his parents profoundly: for Pearl there must have been huge relief that her fourth child was a boy, that the uncertainty she had lived with for six years was now over, and she had done what was required of her – 36 years after the birth of John's eldest daughter by his first wife in 1890, she had given him a boy.

For John, it seems there was almost a sense of disbelief that his long-held wish for an heir had come to fruition. Perhaps this explains why New Year's Eve 1926 was a somewhat austere occasion for the Palace House guests –

> *A great chaff with John as he and I went to bed early last evening and forgot to leave any drinks out!! So they drank neat water to see in the New Year in!!* (1 JANUARY 1927)

'Cares not for man or beast'

Pearl had a knack for capturing moments in her children's lives using just a few words – verbal snapshots that create vivid pictures. One such is her diary entry for 10 November 1927 which is especially memorable –

> *Little kids came down to the schoolroom. Anne sang nursery rhymes with Bunnie and I played with Edward and Caroline. Edward is very independent and cares not for man or beast and fearfully determined if he can't get what he wants at once! He showed the first sign of real temper tonight and lay flat on the floor and screamed!!*

By this time, Pearl was yet again pregnant, although as for her previous three pregnancies, she makes no mention of the fact until May 1928, only a month before the birth –

> *Dr Bott came and saw me this morning – he thinks I am up to time so that my little baby should arrive about June 9th.* (7 MAY)

The pregnancy did not prevent Pearl supervising Elizabeth's coming out, an event that Elizabeth herself would have been happy to avoid. This began with a dance given at Palace House on 3 January – *We weren't in bed till after 4* – and included taking a house in London –

> *The lorry with all the luggage on board left for 22 Egerton Gardens at 6.20 this morning and the Rolls with 4 servants left at 8.50!* (1 MAY)

Both her pregnancy and the demands of London society taxed even Pearl's fortitude –

> *I slept awfully badly last night – in fact didn't get to sleep till after 4.30 so didn't attempt to go to the Chelsea Flower Show at 9.30 with Aunt Netty as arranged.* (23 MAY)

Pearl's diary goes unrecorded for the first week of June and was next written in London –

> *Deluging again early but cleared up sufficiently for Anne to go to the French Institute at 9.30. She was fearfully excited – and came back at 12 having loved it – a little kindergarten class all in French. At 10.30 I went off with Nannie and Caroline and Edward and chose a new pram at Harrods – we will have to have a new one which is made for 2 children – such an expense £20.0.0!*

.... At 3.30 I definitely decided I felt baby pain so told Gravestock [Pearl's maid] *to take my clothes to South Street, telephoned Mummy I would come round this evening. Also rang up Nurse Spencer and asked her to come. Mummy fetched me at 7.30 having written and fixed all plans to the last minute. Had a very cheery dinner, so nice seeing Nurse Spencer again. Wrote to John and went up to bed! Nannie Champ and Gravestock got cot ready, all looked very pretty.* (8 JUNE)

Had pains once an hour through the night but managed to doze on and off and from 6 AM every 10 minutes, and from 7 AM every 5 minutes. Dr Bott arrived at 9.20 and my little baby daughter was born at 10.30 on the 8th anniversary of her daddy and mummy's engagement day but unfortunately not on her daddy's birthday which is tomorrow. I really didn't have a bad time at all, and Dr Bott had left the house by 11.15. I was very disappointed the little person wasn't a son, I did so want another little boy as a companion for Edward. Twenty minutes after she was born Nurse Spencer brought her in to see me. She is very much on the spot and weighed 6lbs 12oz. We telephoned to tell John who was at Beaulieu. (9 JUNE)

The nursery party was now complete, with Nanny Champ in charge –

All the little family came in to see their new baby sister and saw me a minute. Anne was very funny and said she didn't want any more babies at all and that she noticed that whenever I came to stay with Grannie, babies always came. John arrived at 6.45 pm, it's lovely seeing him and I am so glad I got the whole thing over without him knowing it had begun! (10 JUNE)

John was aware of the toll that the year's events had taken on Pearl. His letter to Pearl written after the baby's arrival was signed 'your old man and lover' and contained a request –

And, my sweet woman, to see you today brilliant and beautiful on your pillows after a convulsion, natural but painful, only 30 hours ago was a revelation to your adoring man. You are a wonderful little woman, and you are, thank God, mine. My own dear

Mary Clare Montagu was born on 9 June 1928, the youngest of Pearl and John's children. Her christening on 22 July that year was a *glorious hot summer day*, as Pearl described it. A few days later, the family moved to the House on the Shore as Palace House had been let to tenants. It was the last of the tranquil happy times for Pearl and John.

don't worry your head over anything the next month. Feed and cherish your beautiful babe, and occasionally throw me a kiss and remember me in your prayers. I am only thankful to know that you are safe and past another ordeal, and that the new little life is going to be like you, I am sure, in brain, beauty and soul.

The baby's name was finally chosen –

Still much discussion as to Mary Clare's second name – I rather want 'Mary Clare' – Clare being nearly Mummy's name, Clara. (12 JUNE)

Elizabeth was 17 in September. Academically able, she was very keen to take up a place at Oxford University but the wishes of the more conventionally minded Pearl prevailed and Elizabeth was sent to a finishing school in Lausanne. Changes were afoot and not only for the younger members of the family. John's health was now causing serious concern and Pearl was once more supervising a move to London where he was due to have surgery. But there was some consolation with the arrival of Pearl's old governess, Elizabeth Snushall, nicknamed 'Nooie' –

It is so good of her coming as she has been teaching older children and has not taken entire charge for ages of anything so small as Anne [Anne had just turned seven]. *Fancy it is 22 years since Nooie came to Gladys and me at North House in 1906 when I was nearly 10 and Gladie just 9!* (29 OCTOBER)

Anne started her new life in the schoolroom with Nooie, Miss Snushell, today. Nooie is going to entirely look after her – except Nannie will still have to be responsible for her clothes. Anne is very excited about it! (2 NOVEMBER)

The nursery party was growing up.

Pearl with her young family in 1930, the year after John died. Anne would be the only one of the four children to properly remember her father, something that gave Pearl great comfort. *Anne and I had such a lovely walk down Summer Lane and right along the bank in front of Buckler's Hard. The last time Anne and I came with my darling and Anne remembers every word he said – it is so lovely for me to feel I have one little kiddie who remembers and loves her Daddy as he was – his thoughts and words.* (24 November 1929)

SATURDAY, 15th.

e arrived into Marseilles
harbour at 5.50. Got very
nice letters from the family,
the last before we arrive
home. Everybody up early
dashing about as usual —
but no use — as one cannot get
in the harbour da till after
12!! A horrible strong S.W.
wind blowing — & the dust in
the docks was too awful. At
1.15 Col. Charles, John & I drove
into the town for lunch — wind
just so awful we wished we
hadn't gone — lunched in a tiny
restaurant — & then afterwards
café — for coffee — then we drove back —
arrived at Boulogne at 11

SUNDAY, 16th.
EASTER DAY.

MATTINS—Exodus xii to v. 29: Revelation i v. 10 to v. 19.
EVENSONG—Exodus xii v. 29, or xiv; St. John xx v. 11 to v. 19, or Revelation v.

The boat was not a bit full,
hardly a doz. other people
besides our train. Set up
on deck — as a lovely day. Fairly
rough — by the help of brandy —

MONDAY 17th.

BANK HOLIDAY.

7

SO UTTERLY BEAUTIFUL

Busy with ~~~~ ~~~~ taking ove
cheque books bills etc till we
caught the 12.30 train home
Home Sweet Home again after
~~~~ months abroad. So thrilled
~~~~ seeing ~~~~ ~~~~ ~~~~ again
who ~~~~ ~~~~ ~~~~ months
she w~~~~ ~~~~ when
~~~~ let ~~~~ ~~~~ up a
Brock~~~~ ~~~~ s~~ when
~~~~ arri~~~~ ~~~~ place Hou~~~~
~~~~ foun~~~~ ~~~~ iss if not
~~~~ miss flowers all o~~~~ the driv~~~~
then I took off coats veils etc
~~~~fore I dashed into the inner hal~~~~
found our wee Anne looki~~~~
too devine in Barrett arms,
sitting up. Holding out her
little hands — she was so
friendly to us both — as if
she had known us always — sh~~~~
~~~~ ~~~~ little fairy led h~~~~

CHAPTER 7

SO UTTERLY BEAUTIFUL

✦✦✦

Pearl and John shared a love of travel and adventure. During their marriage they had the opportunity to make two significant trips to remote parts of the world where Britain then wielded power and influence. Both trips illustrate how important social networks and contacts were for the couple, literally and metaphorically opening doors for them.

On Christmas Eve 1921 they boarded the RMS *Kaiser I Hind* (the name means 'Emperor of India' at Marseilles on the first stage of a four-month journey to India. For John, this was a working trip, a chance to revisit a country where he had spent much of the period between January 1915 and April 1919 studying and making recommendations for the improvement of the transport system – road, rail and air. For Pearl, it was a journey of discovery and a chance to spend time with John away from all the demands of home.

The diary shows clearly how Pearl enjoyed and coped with the challenge of new experiences, how she was a ready and supportive companion for John both personally and socially. For her, it seems, this was an India where fairytale became reality, unrestrained and exotic. Her diary gives the impression of a young woman, usually secure and contained in her responses, who found herself confronted with something inexplicable that didn't conform to the rules as she knew them. As a result she simply surrendered herself to the experience.

The couple arrived in Bombay on 6 January 1922, Pearl's 27th birthday - *It is terrible how old I am getting* – and were almost immediately engulfed in the life of British India, a round of lunching and dining, of sporting engagements, shopping and sightseeing. But India was also a place of incipient unrest where the move towards independence was gathering pace. Pearl and John stayed with George Lloyd, the Governor of Bombay who, two months after their visit, arrested Mahatma Gandhi for sedition which resulted in Gandhi receiving a jail sentence.

John and Pearl landed at Bombay in January 1922 and made their way by road and rail to Lucknow and Delhi, eventually reaching the North-West Frontier Province.

After a few days in Bombay staying with George Lloyd and his wife they travelled by train to Lucknow –

> *Woke up bitterly cold – a drop of about 40 degrees. Shivered all night with 3 blankets!! Very interesting to see the Indian life at stations – all huddled together on floor.*
> (12 JANUARY)

> *We motored round Lucknow and went up to see the Residency – the most moving sight – the buildings are left just as they were, after the intense bombardment in 1857-8, standing in a beautifully kept garden and the graveyard – the grave of Sir Henry Lawrence* [see below] *has a lovely wreath of jasmine on it always.* (15 JANUARY)

Lucknow had been one of the centres of fighting during the so-called 1857 Indian Mutiny, a rebellion against the rule of the East India Company. The Residency – to which large numbers of British civilians including many women and children had retreated for protection – was besieged twice for a total of 148 days. Sir Henry Lawrence was then the Commissioner of Oudh and had laid in supplies which enabled the defenders to hold out. The siege and the relief of Lucknow entered the annals of British military and imperial history, the wrecked buildings of the Residency remaining testament to the bitter fighting and large number of lives lost.

By the middle of January Pearl and John were on their way to Agra, west of Lucknow. They travelled on the ancient highway – the Grand Trunk Road – that crosses northern India, running from Bangladesh to Kabul –

> *Got onto the Grand Trunk Road which runs for 1490 miles right across India from Calcutta to Peshawar! A perfectly flat plain with trees either side of the road, making a delightful shade ... eventually got to Agra via Bhongoan and Mainpuri at 6.30.*
> (16 JANUARY)

> *After an early tea, John and I motored out to see the wonderful and world-renowned tomb and garden of the Taj Mahal, itself centred in a beautiful Park. Firstly one passes through a beautiful gate house of red sandstone and through the archway* [one] *suddenly looks upon a gorgeous snow white marble-domed edifice – the approach is by beautifully laid out gardens, intersected by waterways – marble and fountains and either side are planted an avenue of cypress. We walked all round first and looked over the high wall to the*

Pearl took a farewell picture of Sir Edward Maclagan and his wife (front row, second and third from right) when she left Lahore. Sir Edward was an eminent scholar with a great interest in education who founded schools across the Punjab.

[River] *Jumna below – then we entered the tomb itself where the beautiful wife of Shah Jahan and he are buried – all carved and inlaid white marble. We sat in the gardens and looked at it from different lights till 7 when it was nearly dark and all the stars were coming out. So utterly beautiful, it is impossible to understand and describe.* (17 JANUARY)

We left Agra at 10.30 in the car …. Quite straight road the whole of the 150 miles to Delhi. Had a picnic lunch on the side of the road, monkeys and a poor pi-dog eat up our remains!! Got to Delhi at 5, drove straight to Viceregal Lodge, on the top of the Ride where we had tea with Miss Fitzroy and an ADC. Her Ex [Excellency] *Lady Reading sent for us to say 'How do you do'. Then we were taken to the lovely bungalow, 9 Cavalry Lines – all to ourselves – 2 sitting rooms, 2 big bedrooms, two small bedrooms and bathrooms. Roses everywhere here and nice gardens. Found the servants and luggage had not arrived. John and I went for a walk round the lovely gardens in front of Viceregal Lodge, ablaze with English flowers, banks of hollyhocks, beds of roses etc. – too lovely – the sunset was a Turner one – and we saw hundreds of kites flying over to roost over the ridge – as they do every night ....* (18 JANUARY)

They spent three days in Delhi which allowed for some sightseeing, including the construction site that was then New Delhi largely designed by Edwin Lutyens – *a wonderful sight – immense new buildings* (20 JANUARY). Pearl and John then drove to Lahore on the Grand Trunk Road, by now a familiar highway – *dead flat as usual* (23 JANUARY). In one respect Pearl much preferred Lahore – *a wonderful shopping centre – far better than Lucknow and Delhi* (24 JANUARY). She and John were staying with the Governor of Punjab, Sir Edward Douglas Maclagan and his wife, who provided a novel form of transport –

We drove to the Gate of the City, where we mounted Primrose, HE's [His Excellency's] *elephant and rode right through the narrow streets; wonderful old carved wood facades and just tightly packed booths each side, then the road opened out for a beautiful little mosque – only to narrow up again for the continuation of the narrow street. We rode down about 1½ miles, and the people were very civil .... We then came on to the Fort – an enormous walled fortress and dry moat, we left Primrose at the Gate after feeding her with sweetmeats, and got into the car and drove through the archway into the Fort* ... (24 JANUARY)

The next stage of the journey was a two-week tour round the remote region of the northwest frontier, known as the North-West Frontier Province (NWFP) and the border with Afghanistan, where Britain had long faced the challenge of maintaining a military presence. Historically this was the fault line between the two imperial powers of Russia and Britain, and the route by which invaders had entered India since ancient times. By the 1920s the relationship between what was now Soviet Russia and Britain was entering a new phase, but Afghanistan remained strategically important in thwarting any outside move into British India. Britain had fought three wars there, the last one as recently as 1919. That same year, independent Waziri tribesmen had conducted raids against British garrisons and were only suppressed after a 12-month campaign when the fledgling RAF had flown bombing missions.

The Montagus' visit came at an unsettled but politically interesting time that gave John a chance to consolidate his earlier experience in India during the war years; for him this was a tour of investigation as a journalist and transport specialist. For Pearl, everything was new and her diary provides fascinating glimpses of life at the further reaches of Empire where every attempt was made to maintain the cultural fabric. She and John travelled by train in great style.

The railway have kindly given us the most wonderful saloon coach all to ourselves – consisting of a big saloon, bathroom, dressing room with chest of drawers, single berthed cabin, servants carriage and kitchen – real luxury. We went over the Sind Desert today – fearfully dusty – but a dull cloudy day which is very rare – and makes everything much more pleasant. (25 JANUARY)

Arrived at Sibi in the train at 8 a.m. Dull cloudy morning and started to rain and by 2 when we arrived at Mach it was deluging. Colonel Hodgkinson met us there, having motored down from Quetta – we had lunch in the restaurant and then the train started to climb up the Bolan Pass – so sad it was raining so. A wonderful wild rugged pass and the railway is the steepest 'flat' line in the world. Arrived at Quetta at 6 – a wonderful fertile plain after a barren desert. (26 JANUARY)

We have a wonderful Khansamah (cook) on board – we hired him from Quetta and brought food with us and we have marvellous food all cooked in a minute kitchen. We had soup, fish, chicken, wild duck, and veggies, sweet, asparagus, coffee – last night for dinner!!! (29 JANUARY)

We arrived at Darya Khan at 1 a.m. but having our own saloon, they shunted it onto a siding and we got up and had breakfast and did not leave till 10.15 …. DJK is a beautiful oasis in the middle of a desert and the headquarters of the Army for this district. Drove straight to Flagstaff House … (30 JANUARY)

The next morning John went to the Fort at Jandola on the edge of South Waziristan some 70 miles to the northwest. Pearl had to stay behind – *Women aren't allowed to go – which is very annoying.*

Pearl and John then travelled north by road into Waziristan and Pearl saw for herself the limitations of frontier life –

Four Ford cars went off with all our baggage at 10 …. We started off in the Rolls at

N

0   10   20   50
Miles

AFGHANISTAN

Kabul

Jalalabad

Khyber Pass

Landi
Kotal
camp

Jamrud
Fort

Peshawar

Chitral

NORTH-WEST
FRONTIER
PROVINCE

Malakand
Pass

Indus

Grand Trunk Road

Rawalpindi

Miran Shah Road

Kurram R.

NORTH
WAZIRISTAN

Bannu

Jandola
Fort

Wana

SOUTH WAZIRISTAN

Pezu
Pass

PUNJAB

Mianwali

Darya
Khan

TIBET

AFG.

INDIA

11, and passed the convoy just before we got to the Pezu Pass — a wonderful wild rocky lawless Pass where Mahsuds often frequent and then came out onto the fertile and irrigated valley of the Kurram River. Lunched by the side of the road and eventually arrived at Bannu at 4. Drove to the Fort where we are staying ... (1 FEBRUARY)

John, Col Prissick, Major Grassett and Major Geary and Col Hodge motored up the Tochi Valley to Durdoni through Waziri country — women aren't allowed to go which is sad. I wrote letters, and then went for a walk round cantonments. No one is allowed to walk outside the wire netting — so women are so cramped here. Golf course, race course, club, church, 3 shops and railway station are all inside the wire. What a life here for women — but they are all so cheerful. (2 FEBRUARY)

They reached Parachinar on the border with Afghanistan on 5 February. Pearl's arrival was significant —

At 11 we started off to motor to Parachinar, 120 miles right up the Kurram Road. Passed through lovely scenery — at first exactly like the Esterels [mountains in south-east France] *with low scrub and olive trees, and then further on beyond Thall, the Safed Koh range of snow clad mountains come into view. We went all through Afridi country as far as Thall, and then the friendly Turis, every man carries a rifle in this country and we have forts at Thall and Alizai and picket posts of Kurram Militia every so often. We lunched under the watchful eye of one between Thall and Alizai.*

No lady has been up to Parachinar since before the war — but this summer the ladies of the regiments from Kohat are coming up so Sir John Maffey gave me leave earlier .... Bitterly cold when we drove back to the bungalow but glorious moon.

Sir John Maffey was Chief Commissioner of the North-West Frontier Province until 1924 and he and his wife were Pearl and John's hosts in Peshawar after a brief return to Kohat —

We left Kohat at 11 — the luggage in two Fords, for Peshawar 40 miles over the Kohat Pass — a 2000 ft rise in 4 miles, beautiful pass, and the road is cut right out of the rock,

John and Pearl explored part of the North-West Frontier Province (NWFP) starting at Darya Khan in the south and eventually reaching the Khyber Pass. A second trip into the NWFP from Delhi included a visit to the Malakand Pass.

and one rises to the summit where we have a block house and one gets a wonderful view of Kohat below. The rest of the road is through Adam Khel country – but they have to unmolest the road – if they do attack, we punish severely – there are two rifle factories in this valley which we do not interfere with. Every man carries a rifle and belt of bullets – another of our block houses at the mouth of the Pass, and then we went across a plain to Peshawar. We should have seen the snow capped mountain range of Hindu Kush but there was a mist over the City. So warm. Got to Government House at 1 p.m. where we are going to stay with Sir John and Lady Maffey ….(7 FEBRUARY)

There was a trip to the Khyber Pass and a great round of rug buying over the next few days –

A lovely morning. At 9.45 John took me, Miss Sarabji and Miss Williams and an armed Orderly up the Khyber Pass in the Rolls. We went through the fort of Jamrud where the camel caravans have to wait in the Serai, before going up through the Pass on Tuesdays and Fridays. We had a special pass for today …. The Pass is bristling with troops, block houses and pickets on every hill, and camps every few miles, and then we came to the big Fort and camp of Landi Kotal …. then we went on to the Fort, overlooking Landi Khana – the farthest point visitors are allowed to penetrate. (8 FEBRUARY)

…. Shopped with Lady Maffey with the car this morning – after buying 3 more big carpets, a poshteen rug … we have now bought 52 rugs!!! All at bargain prices. (11 FEBRUARY)

Their return to Delhi coincided with the visit of the Prince of Wales who was making a tour of India. Pearl found herself involved in a round of official functions, part of the imperial splendour that was rolled out in his honour. In the event, the Prince's visit was a valediction, the last made by a member of the British royal family who was expected to rule as King Emperor –

I sat next to HRH [His Royal Highness] *… he was fearfully nervous and very difficult to keep up a conversation – we all danced after and several people came in. I danced the first dance with HRH.* (14 FEBRUARY)

At 3.30 we drove to the Fort [the Red Fort] *for the Durbar which was held under an enormous awning – a very wonderful sight with a background of old red sandstone building of the Diwan. 3 thrones for HE* [the Viceroy, Lord Reading], *HRH and Her*

Captain Patrick Grant and his wife, Tiny, were hosts to Pearl and John when they explored the beautiful Swat Valley (now in Pakistan) in 1922. Captain Grant must have taken this photograph of their picnic on 24 February. Pearl noted in her diary that day – *We carried our lunch down by the river which was in spate – so pretty, all the mountains round …. The tribes round here are very friendly – but spend a few months each year going to war with each other across the Valley!*

Ex [the Viceroy's wife, Lady Reading] *were in the middle and then behind them in a long row to the right and to the left were nearly all the big ruling Princes of India in their wonderful native dress and blazing in jewels and pearls. In seats arranged in a semicircle below to the right of the throne were the Legislative Assembly and to the left were the Army Officials, Political, Indian Civil Service …. At 4 Their Exs arrived and then HRH when a procession was formed moving up the Dais. HRH's staff sitting on the right below the Dais and HE's to the left ditto. The Political Secretary asked leave to open the Durbar then HE delivered an address of welcome to the Prince, then the Maharajahs of Gwalior, Patiala and another each made charming addresses and then the President of the Council of State read an address on behalf of the Council of State and Legislative Assembly ….We waited late for the illuminations which were quite wonderful. All the trees, hedges, fountains, water lilies, and railings were lit up and a marvellous waterfall of light all switched on at once when a rocket went off.* (16 FEBRUARY)

The next day there was a polo match – *HRH played quite well for a beginner* – and then on 18 February Pearl and John left to go north to Kashmir, Pearl noting –

We have been made State Guests while in Kashmir which means we pay no bills which is nice. (27 FEBRUARY)

Even in this remote region, the familiar rituals of lunch, tea and dinner held strong –

At 10.30 Tiny [Mrs Grant], *Capt Grant, John and I started off in the car to drive up the Malakand Pass, we went through Dargai Fort and then up the beautiful Pass road – the views over the plain behind us was glorious. Went through Malakand, a dear little fortress town built on the mountain side and then on down the Swat Valley – wonderfully fertile, on up to Chuck Kuder* [sic], *another fortress town on the frontier of Chitral – a glorious day – but strong N wind. Stopped in the fort, and Major Turner in command let us leave our car there – then we carried our lunch down by the river which was in spate – so pretty, all the mountains round. We were taken up to the top of the fort where we had a wonderful view …. The tribes round here are very friendly – but spend a few months each year going to war with each other across the Valley!! They are at it at the present moment. It is in this valley that the famous Swati blankets are made. We stopped at the Malakand Fort on our way home and had tea with Mr & Mrs Tate – he is Canal Engineer here. We went to see the famous Benton Canal opened in 1914 which takes the Swat River through a tunnel of 1½ miles through the mountains and down the Malakand Pass, and thus irrigating all the huge valley as far as Nowshera etc. which otherwise would be unfertile. Got back at 6 after a delightful day.* (24 FEBRUARY)

There was more to come –

The most wonderful drive today I have ever had – right up the Jellum Valley 108 miles to Srinagar – a narrow gorge the whole way to Baramulla where the gorge opens out into the Kashmir Plain – 200 miles long and 50 wide, the road is a wonderful piece of engineering cut out the face of the cliff – often hundreds of feet above the river. We stopped at the Rest House at Uri – a beautiful little place with snow mountains all round us .... we suddenly found the whole Himalayan Range in front of us – the most gorgeous sight – peak behind peak of snowy heights of 20,000 ft, up to Nanga Parbat, 28000 ft, which although 70 miles away, we had the luck to just catch sight of it. A wonderfully clear and sunny afternoon and one might have come up 100 times without seeing it like this – the road from Baramulla to Srinagar is through avenues of silver trunked poplars, planted 2 yards apart .... Srinagar is just a dreamland city ... (27 FEBRUARY)

The next expedition was to Patiala, as guests of Bhupinder Singh, the young Maharajah of Patiala. Once more, they travelled on the Grand Trunk Road (GTR) –

Very warm even at 10 when we left Lahore in the car to motor 215 miles on GTR to Patiala where we are going to stay with HH [His Highness] *the Maharajah .... Very hot indeed and fearfully dusty – we had a strong following wind all the way. Arrived at Patiala Palace at 5.50 – a huge building with beautiful gardens.* (9 MARCH)

Gorgeous day and very hot. HH had to do Holi this morning – Hindu Festival – and went off at 11 and got back at 1.15 – he came to see us before he started in a white muslin dress – he has to be squirted all over with coloured dyes. We stayed in our beautiful suite and wrote. HH came to show us himself when he came back – covered with red dye all over – face, head and body – the most extraordinary sight!! It took him and other members of his suite nearly an hour to get clean .... After dinner the Maharajah had all his jewels out to show me – the most wonderful sight – ropes of huge pearls, 2 huge emerald and diamond necklaces, diamond necklaces, tiaras etc. etc., and the diamond bought by his grandfather from Empress Eugénie of France after the fall of the 2nd Empire, worth then 8 laks!! [an estimated £80,000 in the 1920s].

Then he had all the gardens lit up by electricity for us – what he had done for the Prince of Wales – so pretty and such a lovely night. We walked about for ages. Went and took my dress off and a pearl dropped down belonging to some of HH's pearls – if only one wasn't honest!! It is exactly the size of the centre one in my string!! (10 MARCH)

They had all been hunting for the missing pearl last evening – it was one of the drop ones from the necklace. At 9.30 HH had his elephant in his state howdah and another in his chicari howdah round for me to see. I rode up and down on both .... Arrived at

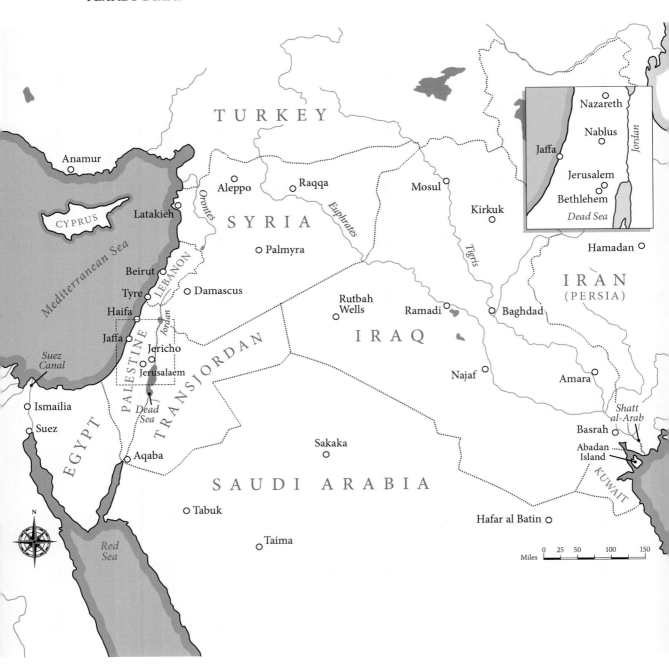

Pinjore at 4.15 — a lovely place inside a high walled garden with terraces of cascades of spring water. We have a nice big room up in the old building. After a rest, we had tea in the gardens and then our kind hosts showed us over the gardens, down 6 terraces, picked some grapefruit and orange blossom and took photos …. A gorgeous evening and then lovely full moon. Had an excellent dinner out of doors and then walked about and sat about in the moonlight, so romantic and wonderful colourings as on the stage. We shall never forget this evening. (11 MARCH)

After a few days in Simla, they returned to Bombay via Delhi and boarded their ship for the journey home after a traditional send-off —

Mr & Mrs Patel (the kind Parsees who lent us their car when we were in Bombay last) were on the dock and put up a beautiful tuber rose garland round our necks and a bouquet of roses each!! Felt like prize bullocks!! (1 APRIL)

'Very good lunch at the Galilee Hotel'

In January 1927, Pearl and John embarked on their second journey outside Europe. The Anglo-Persian Oil Company, later to become British Petroleum, had approached John for advice as a transport specialist, and this developed into an invitation for John to see the situation for himself. The itinerary included a sea voyage from Marseilles to Palestine, a 700-mile journey by car across the Syrian desert to Baghdad, and then a trip southwards to the oil fields at the head of the Persian Gulf. It was a huge logistical undertaking only made possible by the oil company.

As before, Pearl and John embarked from Marseilles, this time on the SS *Narkunda*, one of the P & O passenger ships – 'lovely cabin deluxe with masses of cupboards' – on 21 January. Before they set sail Pearl found time write to Sir Hugh Bell, a neighbour and friend of Violet and Lionel Dugdale in Yorkshire. His daughter, Gertrude Bell, the diplomat, traveller, archaeologist and Middle Eastern specialist had died in Baghdad the previous July.

On 27 January they arrived in Jerusalem after a journal through the Suez Canal from Port Said –

We arrived at Ismailia at 12.15, the beautiful little town which entirely belongs to the Canal Co …. Then we got into the Arrow the fast Thornycroft hydroplane and went

John and Pearl's visit to the Middle East in 1927 included a five-day car journey from Jerusalem to Baghdad.

down the canal towards Suez – 45 miles per hour – such fun and such comfy seats. After tea we had a good rest till dinner, then at 9.30 they took us down to the quay and we got on board the Aigrette and went up the Canal to Kantara [El Qantara]. The hospitality of the Canal Co has been past belief – and we have had a delightful day. Arrived at Kantara at 10.45 and got into our wagon lits for Jerusalem – so wonderful right in to the wilds and find a Wagons Lits. Very tired after a 17 hour day but so delightful.

This was the period of the British Mandate in Palestine after the break-up of the Ottoman Empire in 1918. New boundaries had been drawn across the Middle East as a consequence of the Sykes-Picot Treaty. The 1920s was a period of increasing Jewish migration to Palestine from Europe, with the result that the composition of the population and balance within the economy was beginning to change.

In Jerusalem, Pearl and John found themselves absorbed into a network of hospitality provided by the British colonial administration. Field Marshall Herbert Plumer, one of the most distinguished soldiers of the First World War and referred to as 'Lord P' and 'HC' by Pearl, had been appointed High Commissioner of Palestine in 1925, and he and his staff arranged an intensive programme of sightseeing –

Lord and Lady P gave us breakfast and then we changed and bathed and appeared at lunch at 1.30. After lunch we went off in two cars right down to Jericho and the river Jordan. 1300 ft below the level of the sea – over a mountain road – extremely wild limestone rock scenery. (27 JANUARY)

We walked in the old City by the Jaffa gate. Narrow paved streets with shops each side and we jostled our way through. We walked down a bit of the Via Dolorosa .... We saw the outside of the church of the Holy Sepulchre then went inside the Convent of the Sisters of Zion which is over the old Roman Palace of Pontius Pilate. The sisters took us all over and showed us the 3 perfect Roman arches (excavated in 1860) and the stone slab over them on which Our Lord was shown to the People, Ecce Homo, Behold the Man – then we went under the chapel to the Courtyard where the Roman soldiers stayed and the old pavings are there untouched – and also the real pavements of the Via Dolorosa

The short time Pearl and John (on the left of the picture) spent in Jerusalem in 1927 was packed with sightseeing. They were the guests of the High Commissioner of the British Mandate for Palestine, Viscount (then Lord) Plumer and his wife. On 31 January Pearl wrote – *We all went straight to the Mosque of Omar, the Dome of the Rock. It is really on the site of the old temple. It is quite beautiful and so full of dignity.* The visit was marked with this photograph.

over which our Lord walked — it is now 4ft below the present street level and was covered up with stone debris till 1860 …. At 2.30 we all went off in cars to Bethlehem where we were met by the District Officer outside the Church of the Nativity. The door way in is very small now and one has to stoop to pass through — as the big doorway had to be blocked up as Arabs and their animals used to wander in. The Orthodox Church of the Nativity is the oldest known church in the world built 320AD with massive red marble columns. The District Officer spent his time in telling us of the endless squabbles which take place between the Latin, Orthodox and Armenian Churches, each has part of the church around the manger. We went down into the rock grotto where our Lord was born, the actual spot being marked by a brass star on the ground. (28 JANUARY)

In contrast to her journey to India, Pearl's account of her time in the Middle East does not suggest that she was in any way overawed by the experience, although she was obviously deeply interested by what she saw, especially the religious sites. She was also by now in her early thirties, and confident in her role as John's wife. In her account of this trip, as throughout her diaries, she

The final stages of their extraordinary motor trip across the Syrian desert brought Pearl and John to Ramadi, some 80 miles west of Baghdad. Pearl noted the desert wildlife —*Went through millions of sand grouse — either like a cloud in the sky or acres of them on the ground. They show no fear of cars and don't get up unless we hooted! Also saw thousands of larks. The wild flowers in another few weeks will be too lovely. Stopped for lunch at 1.30 and then on again.* (5 February 1927)

records her contacts with significant 20th-century individuals. One such was Mohammed Amin al-Husseini, a former artillery officer in the Ottoman army in the First World War, who in 1921 had been elected Grand Mufti, the Muslim leader in Jerusalem.

> *8.30 breakfast and at 9.45 we started off in cars to Jerusalem and we all went straight to the Mosque of Omar, the Dome of the Rock, it is really on the site of the old temple. It is quite beautiful and so full of dignity – the actual precincts of the mosque are very large and contains the mosque of Al-Aqsa …. The Sheikh was duly introduced to us and took us all round the mosque – the colouring is quite beautiful – a beautiful gilded iron screen is round the rock of sacrifice and was put in by the crusaders – there are also some lovely Crusader carvings and all the Mosque is covered with splendid carpets … the Grand Mufti entertained us and we drank Turkish coffee and then Bedouin coffee … Later we went to look from a window at the Jews wailing and kissing the outside of the wall and praying and weeping for the past glories of Jerusalem! An extraordinary sight ….*

At this date, tensions between the Jewish and Muslim communities in Jerusalem – including access to the Wailing Wall – were increasing, to culminate in serious and bloody riots two years later resulting in a large number of casualties.

Pearl and John then travelled north by road –

> *Went on the Damascus road through Nablus to Jenin … and then on to Nazareth, 90 miles from Jerusalem – I had no idea Nazareth was so far and to think that St Mary and St Joseph walked all that way to Bethlehem! We had a very good lunch at the Galilee Hotel – clean and run by a German …. Nazareth is beautiful.* (1 FEBRUARY)

> *Such a pretty coast road past the old Phoenician ports of Tyre and Sidon where the main industry is oranges and lemons – about 25 miles from Haifa we came to our Palestine Frontier post run by 2 members of the Palestine Police Force where we showed our passports – then a few miles further on we came to the Syrian Post run by French Syrian Gendarmerie. The road immediately became very inferior – the French have been too busy fighting the Druze to attend to their roads. Hundreds of acres of mulberry orchards, both newly planted and old. Reached Beirut at 2.30 and went straight to the Hotel where we had lunch. It started to pour.* (2 FEBRUARY)

Raining and clouds very low when we left Beirut at 9 this morning. Mr Gerald Nairn came to see us off, also Mr McLean the Manager. Our luggage is following later in the 2nd car. The most wonderful mountain road, both as regards engineering and surface, right up over the Lebanon ranges – it reminds us more of Himalayas around Simla than anywhere else – thousands of houses on the top of every peak belonging to the people of Beirut where they go in the summer – a cog railway goes up too, thence to Damascus – but it takes 12 hours! Got right in the clouds and found snow at the top of the Pass. An enormous wide valley lies between the Lebanon and Anti Lebanon – we took the road to Baalbek – 20 miles – up the plateau 300ft high. (3 FEBRUARY)

We were called at 5.45 and were downstairs packed and ready for the breakfast at 6.35. We started off at 7.10. 7 cars heavily loaded down, 2 ours and two with the mails who go straight through the 750 miles to Baghdad without stopping at Rutbah Wells as the rest of us do! The drivers drive continuously for 40 hours!! Mr Nairn had a telegram for the HC Palestine wishing us to go round by Palmyra, 175 miles further and two sides of a triangle instead of only straight to Rutbah Wells, so we had to conform. French Custom Officials delayed us about an hour before we left Damascus. At a village called Jayrud where we stopped for 20 minutes while the French officer sent a mounted patrol out to the next village – a lot of local ruffians mounted on splendid Arabs – they thoroughly enjoyed racing the cars. Then at a village called Kamakin where we stopped again while 3 cars mounted with machine guns preceded us about 20 kms.

The desert is not sand as we thought, but hard clay soil sparely covered with grass and scrub – rather like Lavender. We had low mountains each side of us all day. This afternoon we had a bit of engine trouble which delayed us a bit. We lunched at the empty hotel at Palmyra, the wonderful Roman Temple City on the edge of the West Syrian desert .... After Palmyra we descended onto the plain which runs for 500 miles to Baghdad, 2500 feet high and absolutely flat, covered with scrub and short herbage. Saw masses of larks and sand grouse. At 9.30 we caught up the rest of our convoy having evening meal over campfires – such a pretty sight in the heart of the desert. A still dry night and the sky a blaze of stars and a new moon. We actually arrived at Rutbah Wells at 12.45 having done 350 miles and been on the road 17 hours. Very tired. Went straight to bed in the rooms inside the fort. (4 FEBRUARY)

The most perfect morning – clear as crystal when we woke and looked out on the desert, 270 miles from anywhere – rather marvellous – just this fort. Dak bungalow in the heart of the desert – built last year by the Iraq government …. We arrived at Ramadi on the Euphrates at 6 PM and kind Major & Mrs Wilson put us up in their charming house – he is District Officer there …. They were great friends of Gertrude Bell and have her spaniel Michael. (5 FEBRUARY)

… we left at 9 and reached Government House, Baghdad exactly at 12 midday …. We have been driving consecutively for 5½ days from Jerusalem – over 1000 miles in all … (6 FEBRUARY)

Sir Hugh Bell … wants me to see about gravestone for Gertrude's grave here … (7 FEBRUARY)

After lunch HE [the High Commissioner for Iraq, Sir Henry Dobbs] *took me in his car out to the big orchards of Hadji Naji, an Arab friend of Miss Bell's to whom I gave Sir Hugh Bell's message. We walked all round the huge irrigated orchard and vegetable garden, right to the Tigris and went to see his oil engine pumping the water over the land. One walks on top of high band between the fields – beans, tomatoes and ancum bass were growing – all planted on the top and between trenches as we grow celery …. went to tea with His Majesty King Faisal of Iraq at his new palace beyond the Iraq Barracks – but as it was flooded out last year, so he is going to have another built later. It is rather a depressing new badly built house, surrounded by date palms … he deplored the death of Miss Bell to whom he was devoted.* (8 FEBRUARY)

We had lunch at 1 with HE and then Capt Clarke took us off to the station. The AP [Anglo-Persian Oil Company] *have kindly given us a saloon coach to ourselves with own cook and kitchen. 2 squadrons of RAF embarked on our train, so General Ellington and crowds of men and a band saw them off on their way to Aden. We left Baghdad West at 2 PM. Very cold and dusty in carriage and found it too shaky to write.* (11 FEBRUARY)

The tour of the oil fields began –

Didn't sleep well. Very cold and rattly train …. arrived at the Barra Camp Station at 10.30 where we were met by Mr Jack, Resident Director of the Anglo-Persian Oil

Company. We drove to their quay on the river Shatt al-Arab (joint Euphrates and Tigris) and board their launch where we had a delightful 2 hours trip down downstream. Date palms on either bank and nothing else – it is the great industry here – thousand of tons of dates are exported per year. Quite near Mohammerah [Khorramshahr, now in Iran] *we turned up the River Karun which flows in on the left bank and there we disembarked at the quay opposite to Mr Jack's beautiful bungalow .... then we went across the river in a ferry and got into cars and drove to Abadan, 8 miles away on the Abadan island which is wholly APOC.* (12 FEBRUARY)

We had to be packed and had breakfast at 9.15 and then ... went up the Karun in the launch to a spot about an hour's run on the left. Here we transferred into cars and started to motor across the desert. We followed the 10in pipeline and telegraph poles most of the way – every 5 miles there is a Persian Line Coolie Camp and every 15 miles a Pumping Station where the oil is boosted up on its way. (13 FEBRUARY)

We have a lovely suite in the Managing Director's bungalow. Mr Seamark and Mr Dunkley live together and it is looked upon as the guest's bungalow. Mr Seamark is Fields' Manager, and Mr Dunkley is Asst Man (Admin). Had 9.30 breakfast and at 10.30 Mr S came and fetched John and me and took us to see the first oil shaft sunk in 1908 'B1' which is mudded down now but left as it was with the old tackle as a museum piece. Then saw the Coz [sic] *fruit and veg bazaar then on to a big seepage place on a stream where we saw the oil oozing out of the stone and floating on the water. Then we went to Fy* [sic]*, the most famous well in the world – 1911-1926 during which time it produced 6¾ million tons of oil. Then on to F3 where they are trying to repair the well by sinking 2 other wells – one either side in order to mud off original well. Then lunch. After Mr D took us to the main stores where we saw ½ million pounds worth of engineering plant and stores.* (15 FEBRUARY)

This was an extraordinary opportunity for Pearl – a chance to see the oil industry as it was beginning to gather pace. In October 1927, a few months after Pearl and John's visit, a large oil field at Baba Gurgur near Kirkuk in British-administered Iraq was found. The strategic importance of oil for both military and economic purposes would have a global impact. Pearl was impressed by the sheer scale of what she saw – *a wonderful sight, vast columns of fire and smoke* (16 FEBRUARY) – but she could not have realised that she was witnessing the early development of an industry that was to have a huge influence on world politics and economics.

Pearl ensconced on a chintz-covered sofa on an open car of a train, most probably just before she and John left Baghdad on 11 February to begin their tour of the oilfields. Pearl recorded although they had a saloon coach to themselves, it was a very cold and dusty journey in what was old Indian railway rolling stock sent out during the First World War.

By 22 February Pearl and John were travelling by tanker down the Persian Gulf back to Aden to pick up their ship for the return voyage. Their last long-distance adventure together ended idyllically –

> *Oh! the kindness of everyone in the APOC, we have had the most delightful 9 days with them, full of marvellous interest. We had a delightful trip down the Shatt al-Arab. The Capt let us sit up on the bridge – just miles and miles of date palms .... Such a lovely sunset.*

JANUARY, 1921.

SUNDAY, 2nd.

SUNDAY AFTER CHRISTMAS.
MATTINS— Isaiah xlii; St. Matthew i v.
EVENSONG—Isaiah xliii or xliv; Acts i.

We all went to church this
morning. Drizzling again.
Mr & Mrs Turner, Colonel & Mrs
Lawrence, Lady Milburn, Angel
Archdale, came to lunch so we
were 15 people & I sat at the
other end of the table for the
first time. After they had
all gone, we went for a
short walk round about.
Dorothy Lubbock came to
stay for the night fr Exbury,
she arrived in time for tea.

MONDAY, 3rd.

A nice day at last. John
Cecil Mr Bremner Col. Luckock
Le Marchant & Mr Greenwood
nephew (Mrs Mrs) went out
shooting, Mum & I went out
in car with lunch, to St Leonards

8
THOROUGHLY AT HOME

TUESDAY, 4th

Poor Cecil Slade had such toothache in the night he decided to motor to London to his dentist, instead of staying with us till tomorrow so sorry he is so seedy & has ... went ... own with ... lunched ... had t ... Miss Knot ... at ... Lymington ... Eliz... called in ... district. We got back at 5. having done good work.

WEDNESDAY, 5th.

John, mum & I went up to London by the 8.50 fr Beaulieu Rd. We dropped John at his office & then mum & I went to see Sir Thomas Parkinson I have been feeling my side a lot since before Xmas —

CHAPTER 8

THOROUGHLY AT HOME

◆◆◆

In September 1918, John engaged a former army officer, Captain HER Widnell, as his land agent. Captain Widnell had been invalided out of the army and he was to spend the rest of his life at Beaulieu. In his memoirs written in 1974, he recalled the occasion when he first saw Pearl in the summer of 1920 on her only visit there before her engagement to John –

> *I saw the most beautiful and entrancing young lady in a coloured striped silk dress standing talking to Lord Montagu …*

Together with Pearl's diaries, Captain Widnell's memoirs provide a good picture of Beaulieu in the 1920s. He understood the nature and strength of the ties that bound John to his home, both place and people, that went right back to childhood –

> *… there was nothing and no-one in and about Beaulieu which, speaking generally, he did not know and love. This remarkable knowledge and affection … gave Lord John the veritable status of a highland chief in his clan, a position which was readily and automatically accorded to him, for he had based all his life on Beaulieu and had passed every spare moment in the Manor, and so had grown up in close association with his contemporaries.*

The depth of these ties is evident in Pearl's diary entry for 31 August 1924 –

> *We heard at 9 this morning that John Crouch died at 5.30 this morning. Too sad – and so sudden. John is terribly grieved, he has been a companion and keeper since John was 19 and they were both exactly the same age.*

'An almost desperate means of earning a living'

Beaulieu was a complex and multi-layered place made up of scattered houses, farms, cottages, the village itself and the community at Buckler's Hard together with Palace House and the

The village and the tenants at Beaulieu turned out in force to welcome John and Pearl as they arrived home on the evening of their wedding day in August 1920, the beginning of a new chapter in the history of the estate.

remains of the former Cistercian abbey. At this date the estate consisted of some 10,000 acres, its boundaries being those of the old monastic manor. More than 2,000 acres were woodland.

The monks had exploited the natural resources of land, forest and river, creating wealth through the sale of agricultural surplus. The wool trade had been especially important for the abbey, helped by the proximity of the port of Southampton. The activities of later lay owners reflected broader external changes – the development of shipbuilding at Buckler's Hard in the 18th century, for example – but whether in monastic or lay hands, the estate needed to turn a profit. It had to be a going concern – many people were dependent on its survival.

An agricultural depression in the last quarter of the 19th century had made farming an increasingly precarious business, due largely to the ready availability of grain from North America and refrigerated meat from New Zealand and Australia. The emphasis was on exporting manufactured goods and importing cheap food mostly from Britain's colonies. The First World War provided a corrective when imports were disrupted by enemy action and the government was forced to intervene. Farmers were guaranteed minimum prices but landowners were prohibited from raising rents. However the boom was short lived and almost immediately after the war farming again returned to the doldrums. Captain Widnell had observed the situation at first hand in 1918 –

> *Farming then, as we all know was on the verge of becoming an almost desperate means of earning a living.*

Pearl was not to know it at the time, but her arrival at Beaulieu coincided with the beginning of the period when inherited estates were to face ever-greater threats to their existence through increased taxation as well as through profound social and economic change.

When Captain Widnell carried out his survey of the estate in 1918, he listed some 25 agricultural holdings, the three largest farms being Beufre, The Park (formerly the Home Farm) and Thorns. The majority of the agricultural tenants were good farmers – Tom Scott at Beufre, for example, was *a man of the very finest type – a first class farmer* – but one or two people struggled. Leygreen Farm was *sinking rapidly* its tenants so hard up *they did not possess any road transport whatsoever, not even a Forest pony and trap*. The tenant at Bergerie Farm was held in special regard – *the great Peter McCallum, doyen of the Beaulieu farmers and much respected by Lord John* while Mr Rowe at Ravensbeck was –

> *... the typical hard-working small farmer of the kind that every landlord liked to see in his smaller farms, for such as he paid their rents with regularity and made no extravagant requests.*

An important part of estate income derived from the shooting rights, and here the interests of the shooting tenants and the farmers could come into conflict as Captain Widnell noted. Mr Lawes at Hill Top Farm was particularly troubled by rabbits –

> *One of Mr Lawes' chief complaints was rabbit damage, and being surrounded by woodland he undoubtedly had his difficulties. Mr Lawes and his confreres were always asking me if they could ferret the Copse Bank. Whatever sympathy I might feel, discipline had to be maintained and although for some no harm might have been done to the shooting tenant,*

Captain Widnell (front row, centre) with the building staff of the estate in 1922 and his fox terrier, Fume, remembered as *one of the very best friends I have ever had.* He was fortunate too in his human colleagues. David Kitcher (front row, second from right) was Clerk of the Works and Head Forester. Captain Widnell described him as *an indefatigable worker with an iron determination, absolute honesty who possessed the kindest of hearts and well-nigh herculean physical strength.*

yet for others it might have proved the thin edge of the wedge .... All I could do was to beg the shooting tenant to do his best to keep the rabbits down, and to point out to Mr Lawes what were his rights over ground game.

Captain Widnell was concerned by the state of some of the land as well as the conditions of the buildings when he began work. He attributed the condition of the former in part to what he called a 'disastrous clause' that had been included in some of the leases 18 years earlier –

The hedges and ditches being bad on entry, the tenant will not be expected to leave them in a better.

Dealing with the results of this was 'amongst my most difficult tasks'.

Similarly, maintenance of buildings had suffered when money was in short supply but especially during the war years when the estate staff had been disbanded and repairs contracted out to a local builder. Many of the men had gone into the armed forces. At a time when agriculture and forestry were still labour intensive activities, the absence of younger workers had been felt.

'Magnificent views across the Solent'

A document that forms part of the correspondence for the marriage settlement between John and Pearl in July 1920 describes an important shift in the composition of the estate that had been taking place under John's stewardship –

... part has been developed in recent years by Lord Montagu as a good class residential property, several houses having been erected some of which have been let on lease, others as temporary furnished houses.

As a result, the nature of the Beaulieu community was beginning to change. In addition to the farming tenants and others who were directly involved with the estate there was also a number of people living or visiting Beaulieu regularly who did not derive their livelihood from it. Some were friends or family connections of John's and they formed a congenial group.

Moonhills House was the first property to be built, its tenant a stock exchange friend of John Montagu. Others included Sir Julian and Lady Orde at Harford House, Sir James Kingston Fowler who built The Vineyards although he later leased it to a tenant, Mr Justice Ridley who built The Rings, Gaspard Le Marchant at Littlemarsh House, Dame Eva Anstruther at Pans Garden and the Armstrongs at Oxley. Sir Thomas Troubridge, described by Captain Widnell as 'number one friend of Lord John', was one of John's regular shooting and fishing companions. He and his wife Laura featured regularly in Pearl's diary. He had long wanted to live at Beaulieu and in 1920 was granted a 99-year lease by John on six acres of land at Hartford Copse in order to build a house. Eleanor (Nellie) Stuart-Wortley, the widow of John's mother's cousin, the painter Archibald Stuart-Wortley, lived on the estate and also became a part of Pearl's life, as did John's cousin, Eddie Stuart-Wortley and his wife, Violet, who lived at Highcliffe Castle. Harry and Rachel Forster lived nearby at Lepe on their return from Australia in 1925.

John himself was responsible for the construction of two important residential properties – the House on the Shore and the House in the Wood. In 1920 both were tenanted. He had taken special care with the House on the Shore ensuring that all the building materials, where possible, were sourced from the estate as described by Captain Widnell –

> *The white bricks from the Beaulieu brickyard, the timber oak for the floors, doors, etc. and natural elm-edged weather boarding for the walls of the upper storey all came from the Manor. The fine old tiles for the roof had come off Thorns Farm Barn nearby, in fact, only the various hardware goods were 'foreign' … the house was long and well proportioned, all principal rooms facing south with a deep verandah which presented an ideal place for sitting out and catching all the sun, and giving magnificent views across the Solent of almost the entire northern shore of the Isle of Wight.*

On her first visit to Beaulieu John had taken Pearl to see these houses –

> *After tea, Lord M took Mum and I and Sir Thomas Troubridge, a tour in the car all round his houses he has built over his property – all too fascinating, all old oak and full of his old furniture.* (5 JUNE 1920)

Pearl was to become very familiar with the House on the Shore staying there on two occasions during the 1920s when John let out Palace House. The first time was in October 1922 when the film producer J Stuart Blackton made his film *The Virgin Queen* at Beaulieu with Diana Cooper

Overleaf: The House on the Shore was built in 1914 in Arts and Crafts style in a secluded part of the estate looking out over the Solent. In the Second World War it was one of ten Beaulieu properties requisitioned by the War Office for training Special Operations Executive agents who were sent covertly into enemy occupied Europe.

in the title role. Elizabeth had gone back to her boarding school by then, but Pearl, John and Anne were to spend nearly two months on the coast –

A glorious morning and so hot – we sat out on the veranda all the morning. This afternoon we took Anne and nurse in the car too and we drove first to see if Lady Diana Cooper was happy at Hill Top which she has taken from us while she is acting as Queen Elizabeth in Mr Blackton's film, then went on to Palace House – they all seem quite happy there. (15 OCTOBER)

Lady Diana Cooper came over to lunch. Most entertaining and peculiar and so made up – which seems such a pity when not acting. (31 OCTOBER)

Palace House was let out again in July 1928 – this time to residential tenants – and the family decamped once more to the House on the Shore for seven weeks.

The Beaulieu Estate – the people who lived there, the people who visited, the events and celebrations that took place – was to thread its way throughout Pearl's diary. Almost more than any other strand, the entries relating to Beaulieu, particularly during her first year there, demonstrate how thoroughly and quickly Pearl became absorbed in her new life –

A nice day but windy. We went to church and Mr & Mrs Reggie Hargreaves came over to church here and then to lunch with us. Mrs H and I walked around the Abbey and went to see Mrs Wortley before lunch. Mrs Widnell lunched too. After they had gone off – John and I went up to the Beaulieu Firs, the tallest English firs in England. Then at 4.30 we went to tea with Miss Hoult at the Lodge – it used to be where John lived when he first married – so nice – then we went for a walk by the river. (17 OCTOBER 1920)

At 1 I went with John to the Audit dinner at the Montagu Arms of all the tenant farmers – I sat next to Mr Malcom and Mr Waters. (25 OCTOBER 1920)

Mr & Mrs Turner, Colonel & Mrs Vanrenon, Lady Millburn, Angel Archdale came to lunch so we were 15 people and I sat at the end of the table for the first time. (2 JANUARY 1921)

Mum and I joined them at lunch at Mrs Robins house (the Head Keeper in Ashen Wood). After lunch she and I went and called on Mr & Mrs Boyd at Newlands Farm on the edge of the Manor at East Boldre. Then to see Mrs Scott at Beuffre Farm, we had tea with her and both farmers wives were so charming and interesting. (22 JANUARY 1921)

John, Mr Hutton, Col Hodgekinson and Tommie went off shooting for the last day of the season – but it poured in the middle of the morning. I joined them at lunch at Clobb Farm, Gilbert Malcom's. Mrs Malcom is very worried as she thinks her little boy of 6 has Scarlet Fever! (31 JANUARY 1921)

After lunch John and I and Jane went as far as Warren Farm and he walked and shot across to St Leonards. Jane and I went and called on Mr & Mrs Bramble, then on Mrs White, St Leonard's Farm where we had tea – then went and watched John, John Crouch and others trying to burn dead grass in Little Buckerleys. (19 FEBRUARY 1921)

After lunch, John, Captain Widnell and I went in the car to see various fields and farms, ended up at Park Farm at the Helps and saw the new engines, coolers etc. they are putting in for cheese making. (15 APRIL 1921)

After lunch John, Tommie and I went in the car to Buckler's Hard, then in the motor boat to Ginns Farm, where we went ashore. We went to see Mr & Mrs Brown and she took me over the lovely old farmhouse. (16 APRIL 1921)

Beaulieu was also the focus for a very diverse mix of people and activities –

A lovely day again which is splendid for the holiday people ... we all went on to Church meadow to the Annual Show of the Ancient Order of Foresters (as Oddfellows). Coconut shies, swings, the usual races etc – everyone the worse for beer. I gave away the children's prizes. (16 MAY 1921)

Very hot. Had 1 lunch and then at 3.30, 80 of the Hampshire Field Club turned up and they went all round the Abbey till 4.30, they all came into tea. A huge party in the dining room. Funny old learned lot of people – archaeologists, botanists etc. Mr [John Frederick] Rayner the great botanist discovered Hisup [hyssop] on the Abbey walls which is the only place in England apparently it is found – so we all went round after tea and were shown it. (9 JULY 1921)

At 3 the aunts, John and I walked up to the Park to the Sports of the RFA Territorials. A lot of people there – excellent tent pegging and then gun carriage drives – they were all marvellously good – when one thinks they've only had 14 days work and mostly young boys of 18. (22 JULY 1921)

At 2.30 the W.I. Aquatic Sports and Fete started and we went and watched the diving and swimming by the Mill – fearfully hot and steamy. I came in and rested till tea. A big thunderstorm started at 4.30 with torrents of rain for half hour, there were excellent side shows in Church Meadow, and tea in the Monk's kitchen. The whole show was splendidly run. At 8.30 they had a dance in the Domus so we hope the W.I. has made a nice lot of money. (20 AUGUST 1921)

Towards the end of 1921, there was a special celebration in the Domus in order that the infant Anne Montagu could be introduced to all the tenant farmers on the estate –

At 7.15 Nurse and I took little Anne over in the Montagu Arms closed car to the Domus to introduce her (aged 8 weeks) to the Tenant farmers and their wives – they were all so delighted to see her and she was quite adorable and smiled at everyone. At 7.45 we all started dinner – run by Mrs MacEntee and Miss Dent and several other ladies waited. John made a speech and then to our great surprise Mrs Bramble, the wife of the oldest tenant of Warren Farm, came up and gave me a case of silver brushes, mirror etc. for wee Anne, from the farmers, wives and lady farmers of Beaulieu Estate. We were so pleased and surprised, it was too kind of them. [3 DECEMBER]

Mines and quarries

Beaulieu had originally been one of three properties settled on John's grandfather. One of these was at Clitheroe in Lancashire which included considerable coal reserves and the largely ruined Clitheroe Castle. John's father had set up the Clitheroe Estate Company as a means of exploiting his mineral rights, and in 1922 Pearl accompanied John to Lancashire. This was more than just a social visit – Pearl had a role to play in the Company –

As John's wife, Pearl (left) was expected to take an active part in local events. The Women's Institute Fete on 9 July 1924 took place in the Beaulieu recreation ground. It was a great success with the two stalls run by Pearl selling out completely, no doubt helped by the weather. Pearl wrote that it was *the most perfect day ... hot and just a breeze.* Nevertheless she took to her bed for the next two days complaining of a summer chill.

John and I caught the 8.40. Jane met us at Waterloo and we drove straight across to Euston where we caught the 11.40 up to Clitheroe in Lancashire. John and I are going up to the audit lunch of the family Clitheroe Estate Co which owns a large area of mines and quarries of NE Lancashire. Mr Robinson, the steward, (he is the 3rd generation who has been steward to the estate) came to meet us and drove us to his house. (8 MAY)

This morning Mr Robinson took John and me down to the Clitheroe Castle where the offices of the Manor of Clitheroe are – shown the room where all the wonderful old deeds of tenure are kept, dating back to 1500 – up to the present day. Then I, as a director of the Clitheroe Estate Co, and John as Chairman, were present at a meeting of the Tenants. Mr Bolton and his son came, also the manager of Sir George Thursby's mines. (9 MAY)

The third part of John's inheritance, Ditton Park, near Windsor had been compulsorily purchased by the Admiralty in 1917 although John still owned some property in the area –

… motored to Datchet where we met Mr Harding, the house agent and we went over John's two manor houses there. Dear old houses about 1500. (22 SEPTEMBER 1922)

Edward's birth in 1926 was especially significant for the estate, an important indicator of its future continuity, an event to be marked –

We had the presentation of a lovely silver tray in the cloisters by Mrs Adams, aged 92, and Mr Sam Biddlecombe representing the 264 people of Beaulieu who subscribed to such a lovely present to the little fellow. (28 NOVEMBER)

Edward's arrival was also celebrated in a different manner at Beaulieu when, in January 1927, he was admitted as a member of the Beaulieu Brotherhood, a society founded by John in 1926 in recognition of the monastic origins of his home. The members were family and close friends, most of whom lived in and around the village. Pearl's mother was listed as 'Mother Superior', Captain Widnell was 'Scribe' and John was the 'Abbot' or 'Prior'. Meetings were conducted with a dinner and, on this occasion, the three-month-old baby was brought down from the nursery to the dining room in Palace House where his health was drunk, along with that of King George.

'An awful woman from Boldre'

By the 1920s, the known and ordered community of Beaulieu stood in sharp contrast to the wider world. These were difficult years as people adjusted to the realities of post-war life with its increasing economic uncertainty and industrial unrest. It was an unsettling and volatile time, and, remote as Beaulieu then was, it was not isolated from political events.

Pearl had a more formal and public role that she was expected to undertake as John's wife, a role that started just a few months after her marriage with involvement in local politics even though at that time she was not eligible to vote as she was under the age of 30. (It was not until 1928 that legislation was passed giving all women over the age of 21 the right to vote.) National and international events ensured that Pearl had a lively initiation into local politics –

At 6.40 John motored me into Lymington to the Women's Conservative and Unionist Association meeting. It was packed. I sat up on the stage with Mrs Whitaker who took the Chair. A wonderful address on Bolshevism and an awful woman from Boldre heckled for Bolshies the whole time. She is a paid agitator. Very interesting …. John sat at the back as it was a Women's meeting. (19 NOVEMBER 1920)

Pearl also lent her support to a number of charitable and welfare organisations. In the days before the establishment of the welfare state and the National Health Service, such organisations performed an important role in fundraising for hospitals, nursing and other services. She admitted to some initial anxiety about taking on a public role –

Bazaar [at] *Southampton to open … in aid of the hostel for Mothers and Babies. Lady Swaythling and Lady Mond and Mrs Dashper (the Hon Sec) were so nice to me. Canon Chitty took the Chair and gave a long speech, then I opened it. I was fearfully nervous and didn't say all I meant to – then Lady Swaythling gave a vote of thanks and then the Vicar of Highfield, then a dear little girl gave me a bouquet of pink carnations.* (23 NOVEMBER 1920)

The Palace House challenge

Almost more than anything else that Pearl encountered in her new life, Palace House itself and its management provided the greatest challenge and the greatest frustration for her. In the 1920s, Beaulieu was a remote rural place, largely self-contained. Changes were beginning to take place but they were slow. Palace House itself had lacked attention in recent years and it did not have the amenities that were then becoming standard in towns and cities. At times Pearl must have felt that she was being left behind in the march of progress, as she notes at the end of 1923 –

We have not got a wireless installation but many houses and cottages in the village, and many houses round have them. (31 DECEMBER)

But the next year Palace House acquired an 'installation' and on Christmas Day 1924, Pearl was able to record a very enjoyable time –

> *Wadley* [the Estate's electrical engineer] *put up our new Burndep 4 valve set wireless this afternoon and we were thrilled. After dinner we danced to the Savoy bands*

On 4 August 1927, George V and Queen Mary were staying in the Royal yacht which was anchored off Cowes on the Isle of Wight for the annual sailing regatta. Queen Mary paid Beaulieu a visit, arriving in John's motorboat at Buckler's Hard where she was met by a guard of honour of Girl Guides. After a whistle-stop tour round Palace House and part of the New Forest, John and Pearl took Queen Mary back to the Royal yacht and were invited on board to meet the King.

in the corridors and Upper Drawing Room .... at 7.30 we dined and Tommie, Laura and Rosemary came and afterwards they danced to the Wireless Savoy Band till 11.15. The servants all did the same as they have a loud speaker in the Hall. A great joy.

In 1926 while Pearl was in London after the birth of Edward she mentioned another life-enhancing technological development –

Rang John up at 9.30. It is so lovely to feel we are on the phone at Beaulieu and it is by my bedside here. So I am going to talk to him twice every day. (23 OCTOBER)

But despite these advances, some essential services were unreliable. At this date the water supply came from the ancient monks' well in Hill Top Wood which provided water for Palace House and most of the village until 1968. The continuing health of this well was of paramount importance as Captain Widnell recalled in 1973 –

... almost reverential attitude which Lord John had towards the Monks Well. Consequently its supervision and care were some of the most urgent and important tasks which he laid upon me, and throughout my time in the Manor Office probably no one thing took a more prominent place in my 'first essentials'.

Just two weeks after her marriage Pearl was introduced to the well –

At 4 John and I went to Col Goodenough's house, Hill Top, and he took us to see Abbot's Well (the wonderful old spring used by the monks hundreds of years ago) and still the water supply for the whole of Beaulieu. (25 AUGUST 1920)

But the source could dry up without adequate rainfall and in the autumn of 1921, while Pearl was in London just before Anne's birth, John reported a problem –

A fearful storm in the night, it lasted about 2 hours, thunder and lightning and torrents of rain. I had a long letter from John saying they were completely out of water at Palace House so I hope they had the storm last night. (12 SEPTEMBER)

Two months later the supply failed again –

John spent all this morning till 2 with the men working hard at the reservoir of Abbots Well – no one has any water again ... I went up and Vincent too, and watched them at work for some time after lunch ... John didn't get back till 6 – very tired. All water has to be carried from the cellar tap. (26 NOVEMBER)

John was up at the Abbots Spring all the morning .... Capt Widnell came to lunch. (27 NOVEMBER)

Mrs Armstrong lunched, still very fussed over water supply as they have none at Oxleys. John worked hard up at the Well all the morning. (29 NOVEMBER)

However, Palace House did have the benefit of electricity generated in the village although this was not able to reach the more distant houses on the estate. One such was the house at Newlands Farm described by Captain Widnell as ... *a good home, but had not much in the way of amenities of a date later than the late 18th and early 19th century.*

'To relieve the establishment'

Pearl was entirely dependent on domestic staff and she was expected to ensure that the household ran smoothly. Her time spent at Crathorne Hall had provided the opportunity to see how a great house was managed thanks to Violet Dugdale's efficiency, and she knew what was expected of a woman in her position. Again, like the work on the estate, domestic cleaning at that date required a considerable deal of physical effort – it was a labour-intensive business.

The first few months of her life in Beaulieu in 1920 seemed to be punctuated with an endless series of servant problems that were difficult to resolve –

Bitterly cold and foggy early. Elizabeth came with me when I went to interview cooks at the Regina. (27 OCTOBER)

The new head housemaid – Cross – arrived. Rather upheavals in domestic quarters but hope all will smooth out – the 2 hopeless housemaids left today. (1 NOVEMBER 1920)

Whiting the parlourmaid fainted before dinner. (2 NOVEMBER)

Mrs Baker our nice old cook left today, Mrs Fairly the new one came last Friday.

(23 NOVEMBER)

At 3 George Sandwich arrived by car having motored the whole way from Hinchingbrooke – he and John went straight out flighting [wildfowl shooting] and didn't get back till 6. Juliet Glyn and Tommie T arrived at 7. Lord Lytton couldn't come down till 6.30, arriving about 9. Had an awful day, as Barbara 2nd housemaid suddenly went away without any warning, with the party just arriving!! Oh! this establishment! (10 DECEMBER)

Cross had another heart attack so had to send for Dr Bird – he says she has strained the muscles of her heart. (21 DECEMBER)

Very busy morning with domestic troubles as usual. Cross is better but mustn't do too much. (22 DECEMBER)

We all had lunch at 1. Turkey, plum pudding and crackers and then the servants had theirs after us and had the gramophone. (CHRISTMAS DAY)

To relieve the establishment, we all except Laura and Tommie, went off in the car at 11 into Bournemouth. (BOXING DAY)

By the beginning of 1921 things had still not improved substantially and she reported –

Still struggling to get servants! (11 JANUARY)

Pearl's maid, Speake, left the next month when Pearl was in the very early stages of pregnancy –

Speake left me today – very sorry to lose her, but she hates the country and goes to Lady Guthrie in London. She went as far as Winchester in the car with my John – who had got to be in London till Thursday .... My first day with Robinson, my new maid – she is very quiet and I think will be good. (14 FEBRUARY 1921)

There seems to have been a big change of staff in 1922 organised by Clara and Jane Clowes, John's secretary, when Pearl and John arrived home after their extended trip to India –

Home sweet home again after 4 months abroad ... went all round the house which looks so nice and clean. Annie and Beatrice must have got it so nice. All new servants which

Mummy and Miss Clowes got for me. Beard, the butler, Mrs Butter the cook, new kitchen girls and new 2nd housemaid – poor darlings they did have a time trying to get a new staff for me. (17 APRIL 1922)

I have got Wilde as temporary maid till I get straight as Robinson is not now coming back to me. Went through all my clothes – found everything beautifully put away. (18 APRIL 1922)

In 1923 there were yet more changes, again after an overseas trip –

Arrived at Southampton. Had breakfast and then went to bed till tea time as felt very overtired after a two day journey. The house is spotlessly clean and Naomi, the new housemaid is so nice and she is very pleased with her 2nd but Mrs Johnson and a kitchenmaid got on Friday so we have still to find a cook, kitchen and scullery, and 3rd housemaid!! Jane has been trying for ages. (17 MARCH)

SATURDAY 24TH MARCH
They [Anne and her nurse] *are coming back to Beaulieu on Wednesday by when I hope to have got a kitchenmaid and scullery maid and 3rd housemaid – what a life!! …. I found Mrs Triggs the new cook has arrived and seems very nice, but still no scullery maid!* (24 MARCH)

In particular, housemaids seem to have been very difficult to find and even more difficult to keep as Pearl noted in 1924 –

Spent all day going over the house with Naomi, very tiring. The new temp Head arrived today – cannot hear of a permanent one. (15 JANUARY)

Naomi and Margaret (head and 2nd house maid) left today – cannot hear of a good head so may have a temp from Mrs Astons. (16 JANUARY)

Caroline with her nanny outside Palace House. Pearl knew well the importance of good nursery staff noting on 12 May 1924 when Anne's first nanny left, *She has been with Anne ever since the month and I can't bear her going, just 2☐years.*

But sometimes events were completely beyond any control as in 1926 –

Fulger [the butler] *in bed with a temp of 102 and was 103 when he waited dinner last night – evidently got flu, Mrs Triggs* [the cook] *is looking after him. Dosing all the servants with quinine and gargling and only hope it won't go through the house.* (29 MARCH)

Find I have a rough throat and head so presume I have caught the cold or flu. Temp was 100 this evening. Nannie got a cold too. Gravestock [Pearl's maid] *took Anne out this morning but when she was rubbing me tonight she thought I ought to know that she had a temp of 101 at that moment – so I said for God's sake go to bed! She is in the room next to mine, so I said she better stay there.* (30 MARCH)

Very coldified. Gravestock has temp, Fulger still 101, and Nannie a cold so via Nellie we telephoned putting off Gladie and Cyril who were coming tomorrow – but Mummy insists on coming this evening with John – although I won't let either of them in my room. (31 MARCH)

Dr Maturin discovered Nannie has a temp of 100 and feeling rotten – insisted on her going to bed. Alice took Caroline and Mummy Anne and things going very smoothly. Mrs Triggs looking after Nannie. (1 APRIL)

Rather a miserable day for me as streaming so – eyes and nose. I can't see to read and just lie with my eyes closed all day. Nannie better after her day in bed yesterday and her temp is normal, insists on getting up and looking after Caroline. Alice (nurserymaid) now down with flu – temp of 102 so sent her back to bed. Mrs Triggs is being splendid and is looking after all ill ones except me. Mummy takes Anne entirely and takes Caroline out too. (2 APRIL)

There was a constant coming and going of servants –

Alice, the nursery maid – left Tuesday and the new one Edith just arrived. Also new butler Taylor came Monday, Fulger left. (7 JULY 1927)

Taylor the butler left this morning and we have a temp parlourmaid. (22 AUGUST 1927)

Sometimes Pearl was called on to be the troubleshooter –

Kathleen, the scullery maid has been so truculent and impossible to poor Mrs Rawlinson, I decided to pay her her week's wage and send her off home, paying her journey! All too tiresome and worrying. (11 MAY 1928)

But one relationship that began when Clara engaged a governess for Pearl and Gladys in 1906, was to endure long after the two girls had left the schoolroom. Pearl recorded the arrival of her new governess at St Leonards less than three weeks after she had first begun her diary, , –

We went shopping with Mum in Hastings this morning and I went to a party at Mrs Wolsy's and I enjoyed myself awfully. When I got back Miss Snushall was there. (17 JANUARY 1906)

Elizabeth Snushall or 'Nooie' as she was called by the two girls – a nickname that stuck – was held in such high esteem that eventually she returned to Pearl at Beaulieu to teach her daughters.

Pearl's diary records the warmth of the relationship with Nooie – an important part of her life even when Pearl was in her sixties and Nooie was living in retirement in Norfolk –

I caught 2.18 from Liverpool Street to Hunstanton to stay with darling Nooie. Her sweet house – all lovely and warm for my arrival … We had a nice little supper together and had so much to say – we didn't know where to begin. (30 APRIL 1960)

Nooie's sudden death just after Christmas 1963 at the age of 85 was a great grief for Pearl. Nooie had been the last link with her own childhood and, as Pearl expressed it, 'someone who stayed with us for all our joys and sorrows'. She had in, effect, been an important witness to some of the key events of Pearl's own life. No wonder Pearl felt her loss describing it as a 'terrible sorrowing shock'. Pearl made the long journey to Hunstanton for Nooie's funeral and then the very next day she went to see Gladys and Cyril –

Went on down to Gladys and Cyril at Edge of the Hill, to tell her about our darling Nooie's funeral. We are both heart-broken – an era has gone for us. (1 JANUARY 1964)

Monday 26 (331-35) John slept well, temp: 99. He feels rather tired after the journey & excitement of yesterday. He stayed in bed till lunch. D' M. came & said he must not walk up or down stairs & his quick pulse is due to weakness & a tired heart muscle. We two had lunch together in the study. Anne, Caroline & Edward all saw their Daddy today they were so sweet. While Jolly rested — looked nurse Anne & I went for a walk — to Hall ford Wood & home by Borman Pond — & saw many beautiful trees down. Poor Ray Pitt. Rivers still in fearful pain — they are having another opinion.

Tuesday 27 (332-34) Another lovely day but bitter N. wind. John had his first bath this morning for 8 weeks! D' Marwich Crisper came to see him says he is to be carried up & down stairs & not to go out yet as his left lung still has a little dry pleurisy & his chest muscles are tired which gives him the hurried pulse

Wednesday 28   (333-33)

9
IN SICKNESS AND
IN HEALTH

Thursday 29   (334-32) John didn't have such
a good night — but temp: normal —
& he thoroughly enjoyed his breakfast
little Edward came along as usual
to "tiddyup" in his Daddys room

CHAPTER 9

IN SICKNESS AND IN HEALTH

♦♦♦

Pearl's diary is particularly interesting in revealing the details of daily life – clear evidence of the extent to which conditions have changed in the past century. One of the most striking features are her accounts of what today would be classed as minor illnesses and the way in which sufferers would isolate themselves until they were well again. This makes sense at a time when there was no effective antibiotic treatment available and a cold or influenza could develop into something far more serious and possibly even life-threatening. Pearl's diary gives the impression that good health depended above all on being cautious and taking serious account of symptoms which later generations, cushioned by the effects of pharmaceutical and medical research, would usually dismiss as being trivial.

But this caution was simply a reflection of the reality of the world into which Pearl had been born, a world where there were far fewer comfortable assumptions about health and medicine and where most medical care happened at home, if at all. Compared with today it was a far harder and more dangerous world in many ways, even in Britain which was at the forefront of industrial development. However, industrialisation and the consequent expansion of the urban population in the 19th century had created densely packed cities where public health had lagged behind. When Pearl was born the science of bacteriology was still in its infancy and the number of people dying from infectious disease was far greater than it is now. In 1901, life expectancy for boys at birth was 45 years; for girls, it was 49. For every 1,000 children born at the beginning of the 20th century, 140 of them would die within the first year of life.

A typical example of the attitude towards illness at the time is Pearl's description of a week at the beginning of 1909 when she was 15 and living in St Leonards with her parents and Gladys –

Pearl (left) and Gladys with their nursemaid in a photograph probably taken shortly before the family left Chawton in Hampshire in 1901. The sisters enjoyed all the advantages of a solid middle-class family life with access to medical care if necessary, and the benefits of long holidays in the country at their Aunt Violet's house in Yorkshire.

We had our French lesson today. Dad is in bed today with a bad cold. (18 FEBRUARY)

Dad is still in bed today. (20 FEBRUARY)

Dad got up in his room today. (22 FEBRUARY)

Christmas at Crathorne in 1913 was another such instance –

A glorious day. Gladys stayed in bed because of her cold. After church Uncle L took us round the farm etc before lunch. Maurice Bell and Mr Marshall came over. I stayed in and sat with Gladys this afternoon. (21 DECEMBER)

Gladys stayed in bed again today …. Aunt Vi, Beryl and I went in the car to Darlington to finish Xmas shopping. (22 DECEMBER)

Gladys' cold so heavy she did not come down to dinner. Beryl dined down and we all danced after. (CHRISTMAS DAY)

At this date, good health care was dependent on means. In 1913 Aunt Vi had an operation for appendicitis, carried out by the celebrated Australian surgeon Sir Douglas Shields in his private hospital –

Went to Aunt Vi's Home in Park Lane (next to Londonderry House) to see her. She is very calm and I think quite relieved that they want to operate for appendicitis tomorrow as she has had such pains and felt so seedy for ages. Sat with her for a long time. She has a lovely room and is so comfortable, it is such a lovely home, just like a private house. (30 SEPTEMBER)

Aunt Vi was operated on for appendicitis at 9 by Dr Shields at 17 Park Lane. Fripp and Vernon Jones were there too. Mum and Uncle L went there about 10. Saw the surgeon after who is very pleased, they found an adhered appendix, she stood the operation well.
(1 OCTOBER)

Despite the age gap of nearly 30 years between John and Pearl, John's energy more than matched that of his young wife. Pearl, however, would not hesitate to rest when she felt she needed to and her diaries often refer to days spent in bed. By contrast, John drove himself very hard and was extremely reluctant to admit any physical weakness or fatigue.

Pearl's strong constitution and stamina were to stand her in good stead in adult life when during her marriage to John she gave birth to five children in seven years. The diary for the weeks following Anne's arrival on 3 October 1921 show how markedly medical and social attitudes to childbirth have changed since then –

Very good night. 15 telegrams came in yesterday for John and me and endless letters though not seeing them yet as keeping very quiet. (5 OCTOBER)

At 4.30 I got up for first time, found & put on a few undies and dressing gown and sat in armchair for tea. Felt very shaky on my legs – stayed up for an hour. (22 OCTOBER)

I got up this morning and dressed for the first time and went downstairs in the drawing room before lunch. (27 OCTOBER)

'A touch of fever'

One disquieting note sounded from time to time throughout Pearl's marriage to John that was first heard during the days of their engagement when she was convalescing from her appendix operation –

My John arrived armed with flowers, vegs, eggs, chickens etc. at 2. Very seedy poor darling – he has a touch of fever ... he sat with me till 7.30. We were very peaceful – he in a comfy chair, he had a temp of 100 degrees when he went off to dinner with Gladys, poor darling. (28 JUNE 1920)

John suffered from asthma and Pearl describes a severe bout while they were on board ship at the beginning of their first long overseas journey together in 1921. One asthma treatment at this date included burning medicated powders and inhaling the smoke, something that John evidently did. This attack was evidently very severe and must have been an intensely miserable and debilitating experience for him –

A strong following wind which makes a slight roll .... Poor John had asthma last night and is a bit wheezy today. (24 DECEMBER)

On Anne's christening day on 6 November 1921 Pearl wrote – *I fed my little Anne for the last time at 12.45 today – too sad but Nurse says it takes so long to get rid of one's milk and I simply must get strong with so much to do before India .... I found I was fearfully tired as I stood so long today so went to bed before tea, and did not get up for dinner.*

Poor John has asthma all last night so could not come to early service with me. (CHRISTMAS DAY)

John was very bad all night poor darling – sitting up most of the time and burning his asthma powders. He had to stay in bed all day. Still cold and rough. It is too annoying about darling John. (BOXING DAY)

John had another bad night, poor darling and had to stay in bed all day again or just in his chair in the cabin. A bit warmer today. This evening there was a Fancy Dress dance on deck ... too sad John couldn't go. (27 DECEMBER)

Pearl's diary gives the impression that it was John's determination and force of will that kept him going in spite of bouts of illness, and at times when he must have been feeling well below par. Although he probably did not suffer more minor illnesses than average given that he was asthmatic, he may have had a greater exposure to infection due to the extent he moved around between London, Beaulieu and elsewhere. He evidently tried to ignore illness as much as possible in contrast to Pearl who was careful in looking after her health and would spend days in bed when necessary. John's determination to soldier on even when he was evidently unwell was apparent to Pearl as early as February 1921 –

John still got a bit of a fever and feels very seedy and I was very tired after yesterday – so we both stayed in bed till nearly lunch. He had to have 1 lunch and dash off to a political meeting in Southampton at 1.45 so bad for him feeling like this .... John got back at 4.30, very sad for himself and then had to have a Parish meeting at 6.30. (5 FEBRUARY)

But this didn't stop John and Pearl embarking the following day on the first of a series of motoring trips commissioned by *The Times* to look at Britain's road system. The second of these trips began later the same month and ended badly –

John feeling very seedy from his cold – had to leave here in the car to catch the 11 train to London as he had to attend the lunch given by Rolls Royce to the two Smith Brothers who flew to Australia, then this evening at 7 he had to go to the Hygenic Institute Dinner – but was feeling so seedy he went in morning clothes and only stayed till 8 and caught the 8.30 down, arriving home more dead than alive at 11. Poor darling, felt it was his duty to go up today – but it was madness. (3 MARCH)

This was one of the instances in which an apparently minor complaint developed into something more serious and even John had to concede that he really was ill –

> *Found my John's temp is up again to 101.4 – too maddening – he allowed me to send for Dr Maturin.* (7 MARCH)

On this occasion John was suffering from what was believed to be paratyphoid B or, in the view of his old friend, Sir James Kingston Fowler –

> *... a bad form of gastric flu going about.* (23 MARCH)

Nevertheless it was extremely debilitating and it wasn't until the end of the month that John felt better and his usual energy returned.

In 1924 a bout of bronchitis laid him low and delayed his trip to the south of France with Pearl. It was a wretched time for them both especially as they were staying in a hotel. A one-night stay at the Grand Hotel, Folkestone before crossing the Channel expanded into an unplanned 15-day visit –

> *John's temp still 99 early – very miserable. Dr Lewis came and wants him to try and keep quieter today and only drink milk. It is all so disheartening – he is not so well as at the beginning of the week. John's temp was up to 101.2 at 4.30 again. Of course he ought to be in bed but can't lie down because of coughing.* (1 MARCH)

'So weary'

John was predisposed to respiratory infections but by the autumn of 1928 it was evident that something very serious was wrong. Pearl refers to 'cystitis trouble' in September and at the end of the month notes –

> *My poor darling had a shocking night – so stayed in bed till late. He is so weary with continued bad nights and looks so CD* [seedy]. (28 SEPTEMBER)

In her 2003 autobiography his daughter, Elizabeth, remembered this period of John's ill-health –

Despite his huge energy and capacity for ceaseless work, my father's health was now in decline. The concerns which my mother felt for her husband over ten years before were now becoming apparent to Pearl.

In October John saw a specialist –

He went to see Dr Thompson-Walker the specialist who thinks John will have to have the prostate operation sooner or later and really the sooner the better – he found his heart and lungs and blood pressure is in very good order. He says the continual thirst and other discomforts are all caused by the enlarged gland – finally brought to a head by a chill. (10 OCTOBER)

On 16 January 1927, Pearl wrote in her diary – *A glorious clear winter day – perfect for taking the Kodak Cini-film. After church John took me coming out of the house with Edward and Anne and Caroline running along – then Anne throwing a ball about and then Jane [Clowes] took the film so that John could be in one. I do hope they come out.* These stills from the film taken by Jane were later to become very important to Pearl when she lamented that she had so few pictures of John as he was usually the person behind the camera.

The operation was due to take place before Christmas in London and the search for a suitable house to rent for Pearl and John began –

> *John and I went to see Princes Gardens and Eton Square houses and we went and made an offer for 4 Princes Gardens from Monday November 5th for 6 weeks.*

On Sunday 21st heard that 4 Princes Gardens is withdrawn from the market. Too maddening as can settle nothing. (18 OCTOBER)

On 1 November the problem was resolved –

Mummy met me at the Hyde Park Hotel at 12.40 and I met by appointment Sir John Thomson-Walker and his special nurse and we went up to see the rooms on the 3rd floor. A lovely big bedroom, bathroom and big sitting room which they will turn into a bed sitting room for me. We went into the question of lighting etc with the electrician – things I should want with Nurse and then saw the housekeeper who said she'd see to everything. John went up to the London so that treatment before the surgery could be carried out.

Preparations for surgery began –

John had a good night and is cheerful this morning but Sir John TW came and did a more serious and painful treatment which was very painful and exhausting for him. (14 NOVEMBER)

But a secondary condition delayed the operation and after a number of medical specialists had visited him, John returned to Beaulieu –

John had a fair night and cheerful this morning – he feels the operation will be on Wednesday. The poor darling is longing to get it over. Sir J T Walker came at 10 and depressed him very much as wouldn't commit himself to any date .... Owen Seaman came to see John at 4.30 and Col Hacking at 5.45. It was a bit too exciting for him. Sir J T Walker, Dr Young and Dr Ingram came at 7.30 and had a long consultation and eventually at 8.20 came into see me. Sir John spoke first and said that the blood iron tests had not come out sufficiently well for him to contemplate operating yet – and then Dr Young said that he had a small patch on the base of his left lung – purely from being in bed for a fortnight and that that must be cleared up before they would dream of operating – so together they propose that John should return to Beaulieu one day soon – and have a male nurse expert in the catheter job. Of course it is a fearful disappointment to my darling – he had so hoped for the op to be done on Wednesday or Thursday. They will not settle definitely till tomorrow morning. (19 NOVEMBER)

Home again, [to] Beaulieu. John slept well and temp 99. He feels rather tired after the journey and excitement of yesterday. He stayed in bed till lunch. Dr M came and said he must not walk up or downstairs and his quick pulse is due to weakness and a tired heart muscles. We two had lunch together in the Study. Anne, Caroline and Edward all saw their Daddy today – they were so sweet. (26 NOVEMBER)

Another lovely day but bitter N wind. John had his first bath this morning for 3 weeks! Ted Crispin came to see him. Dr Maturin says he is to be carried up and downstairs and not to go out yet as his left lung still has a little dry pleurisy and his heart muscles are tired which gives him the hurried pulse. He is ever so much better in himself – though of course gets tired easily. He came into the dining room for luncheon today. (27 NOVEMBER)

John had a good night and usual morning sub normal temp which makes him feel very depressed. Dr M gives no idea when this lung will clear up, which is so depressing for him. (6 DECEMBER)

A lovely day. John was out in the Abbey and Garden by 10.30 …. This afternoon John and I went down to Warren and walked along the shore. (20 DECEMBER)

Another nice day. John was out this morning and afternoon. We went down to see Gaspard at Little Marsh and he had quite a mile's walk along the bank. So gloriously fine. (21 DECEMBER)

John came down to breakfast for first time since he has been ill. We went to church at 11 and then John joined Helen and me for Holy Communion at 11.45. It was so nice he was well enough to come. (CHRISTMAS DAY)

For a few weeks a semblance of normal life was resumed, with John even able to go out shooting and make a brief trip to London –

Cecil went off shooting at 9.45 and John followed at 11 and shot for the first time today – bitterly cold so I do hope it won't do him any harm. Helen and I went out with the lunch and I watched the stand in Ashen Wood before lunch. John shot so well. He came back after one drive after lunch. (31 DECEMBER)

Here is another year. May it be an easier and happier one than 1928 – which was so full of illness and worry and may my darling get stronger after his operation. (1 JANUARY)

Mummy and John and Reed up to London by 9.34 – Mummy for the day and John returns tomorrow. I do hope it won't make his cold worse – but he will go! (16 JANUARY)

John had tea and then caught the 5.5 to London. He stays tonight at South St and returns with Cyril tomorrow. I hope it won't make his cold any worse going to London. (22 JANUARY)

John's last day at Beaulieu included a walk with Pearl to Culverley, a much-loved place –

The most divine day, 26 degrees of frost and mixture of St Moritz and Riviera – quite hot in the sun. Little Caroline went to church for first time. She was so good. 1st Sunday after she was 4. The same age as Anne went. Had 20 mins skating on Church Pond before lunch. After lunch John and I went by car as far as Culverley and then walked through snow as far as Beaulieu Road – then back through La Ferme Croft and Culverley – went in to see Mrs Kingsmill Coke, a few minutes. The Rolls joined us there – we then walked home across the Mill Dam. (17 FEBRUARY)

John, Read and I went off by the 2.2. It is nearly 3 months since we returned from London and ever since we have been expecting for John to go up to London for the operation but first he had to get well after the pleurisy, then he caught flu, then Miss Lancaster couldn't give him a room. Now at last he has his room in 29 Wimpole Street. My darling is so much better in himself now and his nerves are so rested. (18 FEBRUARY)

I breakfasted at 8.45 ... then went off to 29 Wimpole Street to see John before Sir John Walker arrived. I spent the morning in and out of his room. Sir J was very pleased with him – and then Shipway the anaesthetist came and sounded him and says his heart and blood pressure 125 is very good for an operation. Sir J Walker has decided to operate at 9 AM tomorrow morning – One feels so glad for my darling's sake as well as mine that the waiting about since the beginning of November is nearly over. (19 FEBRUARY)

The operation of my darling John at 9 at 29 Wimple Street for Prostate Gland. I breakfasted at 9 ... then walked to the Home, arriving at 9.50. Nurse Shaw met me at the Hall and said Sir John Thomson-Walker said the operation was satisfactory. I then saw Dr Shipway, the anaesthetist who said he took the anaesthetic well. They gave him Novocain injection in the spine and then very little chloroform and ether .... Sir John and Reggie Ingham came down at 10.10 and said the operation was most necessary, difficult but he had stood it well and his condition was good .... I went to the home at 4 but he had been restless, so they gave him some more morphine. (20 FEBRUARY)

Found John had awful night. Sir John was with him till 12 and Mr Andrews till 3, and they had to get hold of Reed to help and Miss Lankaster and Nurse were there too – trying to keep him from throwing himself about. They were so terrified of haemorrhages. However his wound is none the worse and his pulse is good. Very restless all day. Spent most of the day at the home. (21 FEBRUARY)

The next few weeks were deeply anxious and distressing ones for Pearl as she watched John's suffering – she described it afterwards as 'mental agony'. His condition fluctuated but at the beginning of March he showed an improvement although there was also a sign of his old complaint – bronchitis.

Went off at 9.15 as usual. So mild but a bit foggy. Saw Sir John who is very pleased with the wound and says my darling is slowly mending. His digestion is better though he is so tired out .... My darling is a bit bronchial today so we had the steam kettle going – we do hope his lungs won't get congested again. (7 MARCH)

Went by taxi to the Home by 9.50. Found my poor darling had a bad night .... This wretched bronchitis ... (10 MARCH)

On 14 March John's sister, Rachel Forster, who was all too aware of the gravity of John's condition, wrote to Pearl from France –

Overleaf: The last family photograph taken before John went to London for surgery in February 1929. John's final days at Beaulieu coincided with an intensely cold period of weather. Pearl noted that the Mill Dam was frozen over, the first time since 1895.

I know how wearing it is to see people ill & suffering & you have had such a long time of anxiety on & off – Please give him my love & sympathy. I do hope soon for a better account. I would send a wire to ask but fear to worry you. I shall be quite content with a post card if you are too busy ask Jane or Helen or Elizabeth to send me one. Don't worry darling about writing yourself – though of course I always love your letters – but I know you have so much to write & think of & are probably helping to nurse John. You would have been pleased & proud to hear the way he spoke of you that evening I saw him last – he said you had been simply wonderful in your sweetness and helpfulness all through his illness – and how you had kept him going with your cherishing and sympathy and love. He wondered how he could ever have deserved such blessings as you had brought into his life. Long may he be spared to enjoy them!

Two weeks later, the doctors treating John were certain what the underlying cause of his illness was –

My darling has a restless though fair night …. Dr Young and Dr Ingham came at 10. Dr Y says my darling is 'holding his own well' but he wants to come again tomorrow to discuss the X-ray photo as they feel sure there in an abscess in the right lung – which accounts for the continued rise of temp. (25 MARCH)

Dr Young and Dr I came at 10.30 – both definitely decided Mr Tudor-Edwards (the big lung surgeon) must be asked in, in consultation and see photos which definitely show an abscess. (27 MARCH)

Mr Tudor-Edwards and Dr Ingham and Dr Young came at 8.30 and Mr TE operated on my darling's left lung and found a large abscess which he opened up and put tubes in. His condition is grave – but his heart stood it – and today they want him kept as quiet as possible. (28 MARCH)

Went up to my darling where they were trying to get him to drink – but it is awful – all persuasions seems to fail. Oh! he looks so ill, it is heart breaking. Pray God to give him strength. (29 MARCH)

Nurse Crumpler came down to see me at 7.40. She looked very grave but said they had managed to get 1½ pints of fluid down by saline injection during the night and some

Vichy – pulse up to 136 and respiration up and temp 100.4. I was very missy and worried .... the doctors came at 10 and suddenly Staden rushed in and said you know your husband is terribly ill – you realise it don't you!!, and then left, and then dear Miss Lancaster came in with brandy and water and was so sweet to me – but it was all over upstairs – my darling has gone, he couldn't fight anymore after 5 weeks 4 days, and this dreadful poison was too much for his heart, and has been so awful fighting on – till this abscess and the fearful poison must have reached the heart – because quite suddenly in the middle of Mr Tudor-Edward doing the dressing he had a heart attack and died! He was not conscious and it was all over in a second. Oh! the mercy of that – but oh! oh! oh! .... My John had been really my only thought for years – we have been as one.
(30 MARCH)

'Beaulieu material and Beaulieu labour and Beaulieu love'

That night Captain Widnell accompanied John's body back to Beaulieu. The following afternoon Pearl was driven home by her cousin, Tom Dugdale, in company with Harry Forster –

Tommie Dugdale motored up from Bournemouth especially to motor me down – so Harry, Tommie and I started off at 2. The most glorious day and so clear. It was nice him motoring me down ....O! such a day for my return – not our return – it's been our everything for 8 years 8 months and now – oh! God help me. Helen and Eliz met me and then the darling old Vicar met me upstairs in the beautiful upper drawing room and we cried together in the Anti room and then we went into the most beautiful sight. My darling's body (he is gone and happy in heaven) covered by the big white ensign with 6 tall oak candles – the brass cross on the table behind. Masses of azaleas (sent by Leslie Scott) and a white hyacinth given by Nellie and then just Rachel's wreath – and my wreath of white lilies and all the lovely lilies given by Harry in the East Window. The sun pouring in and windows open. What a setting – and how he would have loved to have been brought there. We said our prayers and the darling old Vicar blessed me.
(31 MARCH)

A glorious day and much warmer. After breakfast I saw Aldridge re marking a beautiful cross of Beaulieu daffs to go the full length of my darling's coffin. Tommie came across from Bournemouth and at 11 he took Harry and me to see the Bishop of Winchester at Wolvesley Palace by appointment. I asked if he would give a short address and explained to him how the Vicar so wished to give the Blessing! He was very sweet and consented but it was a brave thing to ask! I let him read my darling's wishes with the words he wished put on his grave and the Bishop is going to make his address around my John at his Beaulieu. At 3.15 Tom sent me and my 3 darling babes for a drive round by Lepe, Fawley and Hythe till 4.45 during which my time my darling's lead coffin was encased in a beautiful Beaulieu made oak coffin with iron handles and iron name plate and a beautiful wooden cross down the centre – just what my darling would have loved – everything simple of Beaulieu material and Beaulieu labour and Beaulieu love. At 6.30 5 groups of 8 men, each drawn from the different sections of the Estate – such as woodmen, keepers etc. came and they carried his precious body down the main stairs and out of the front door. Harry, Rachel, Mummy and Helen followed as far as there – then Mummy, Rachel, Harry and I went across to the church.

Such a lot of his beloved people came – and we had a beautiful little service and then when I left I knew that 4 watchers in relays of 1 hour each were going to stand at each foot of his coffin – all through the night!! So beautiful – all volunteers and 54 people offered and couldn't take part! Dor Pease and little Jane and Mr Nichol our lawyer arrived down at 7 by the 4.30 bringing masses of beautiful wreaths. I stayed in bed for dinner, so did little Ma. Tommie Dugdale stayed the night – oh! he has been so wonderful helping Harry and Widdie. (2 APRIL)

My beloved darling's funeral day in his Beaulieu which he loved so well …. At 12.30 Harry took me over to the church – which was a perfect sight – entirely decorated with wreaths. All the window arches, front and columns up to the pulpit. Rachel and Dor came too and we put all the family wreaths (and little basket from the children) quite near my darling's coffin which stood on a wheeled bear, with 6 lit candles. Oh! his church looks so beautiful and he wouldn't have wanted anything more beautiful – to have been buried in his Abbey on a Spring Day by his people. Went over to see the grave which is 7ft deep and lined by Aldridge with moss and daffs and all inside the little Burial Ground were banks of wreaths. Quite, quite beautiful.

The church was packed. The choir came in to 'Lead Kindly Light' and the Vicar walked behind the Bishop of Winchester and he sat in a special seat left of the altar. Jack Seely in a special seat in front of and end of our front pew as Lord Lieutenant. The dear old Vicar Daddy Powles and Tubbie Clayton took the service and then the Bishop gave the most beautiful address 'Progress and Peace' was his main theme and said the most beautiful words about my darling, just what I wanted. Sang all through the service and got through it without a real tear – it was all so uplifting and I felt my darling is so happy. We went out to the Nunc Dimittis and then sang Hark my Soul! Only immediate family came inside the little burial ground and the choir sang in the Chapter House. After the committal the darling old Vicar said the Blessing. John will be so pleased and then Abide with Me …. I went to bed at 7. Very very tired. Never felt quite like it before. I felt pins and needles and felt as if I was falling through the bed! (3 APRIL)

'Unable to pull him through'

A letter survives to Pearl from the surgeon, Mr Tudor Edwards, which throws light on her enormous courage and self-discipline. It is evident that even under conditions of extreme stress and anxiety, and in shock from the loss of her husband, Pearl nevertheless had found the time and energy to write to Mr Tudor Edwards immediately after John's death. She evidently felt that in some way she had been discourteous to him. His reply was swift, dated 1 April –

Dear Lady Montagu

It was extremely kind of you to write me in the midst of your trouble and quite unnecessary for you to apologise for any seeming rudeness. Frankly, I had not regarded it in any such way and fully realised the enormous mental stress for you at that time; naturally, I feel that Dr Ingram would be able to console you far better than was in my power to do.

I am sure you will realise how very grieved I was at the somewhat sudden heart failure but there is no question but that he made a tremendous fight and that only a strong man could have survived long.

I send you my most sincere sympathy in your great sorrow and my great regret that we were unable to pull him through.

Thurloe Sq

Edward came into my bed at 7.30.
We looked at a Puffin train book.

On this Saturday
year ago little Mary Clark
was born here in Mummy's house,
tho' her actual birthday (9th) is
tomorrow. Oh! to think of the
happiness around me then — but God
has been good to give me all his
little kiddies & tho' at the time
I didn't really expect or want them
Clare — the little darling will be such
a toy to me — his little last born. She
was only 8½ mths old when her Daddy
died. Poor wee tiny will never remember
you. Was out by 9.15 & got by car
10.30 & spent all the morning at
2 helping her with this after
uproving of & books & files it is so
difficult to know what to keep

what to destroy. It is a cruel work
for poor little Jane — her life's
work all gone. Very tired & messy
when I arrived at lunch at Aunt
Nellys. Sommie trugdale was there

Monday 10 (161-204)

10
WORTHY OF SUCH A TRUST

My beloved birthda[y] ... years ago since I gave him his first present (the note case which he used till the day he died) ...

Tuesday 11 (162-203) S. Barnabas.

...birthday to day — fearful excitement of Anne. The most perfect day. Aunt Hetty has hired a car for all my children ...

CHAPTER 10

WORTHY OF SUCH A TRUST

◆◆◆

The days after John's funeral were almost unbearable for Pearl. Her own feelings of desolation and grief were a deeply painful contrast to the knowledge of the huge task that lay before her — a task that would require all her energies —

> *Slept all right till 6.15, that time before I am called at 7.30 is so awful. The overwhelming sorrow and the fearful feeling of inadequacy but buoyed up by his complete confidence in me. May God help me to be worth of such a trust and may I live to bring up my darling's little tinies as he would have wished …. My nerves are very jagged after my 6 weeks anxiety and mental agony and now these last 6 days of strain. I feel myself I must rest as I am not fit now to take up so big a responsibility. My little wee Sonnie only two — but so precious, Caroline aged 4 and my babe aged 9½ months and my darling Anne aged 7 happily away at Hindhead with darling Nooie and Gladie.* (4 APRIL)

She was physically and mentally exhausted —

> *Dr M wants me to stay quiet in bed for 3 days and rest my whole nervous system — which has had such a strain and I know my darling would wish it now I have no one really to definitely settle for me. My darling little Ma, Harry and Rachel are all doing their very best to help — but the void left by the departure for ever on this earth of a vital personality such as my John who adored every little bit and thought of me and I who really only thought of him — he came absolutely first in all my thoughts for 8 years 8 months* (5 APRIL)

It was at this crisis in her life that Pearl's remarkable mental and emotional strength becomes so completely evident. She may have been drifting in the wreckage of her previous well-defined

Something of the anguish that Pearl endured in witnessing John's final illness and her subsequent vulnerability and confusion, is visible in her face in this photograph taken a few weeks after his death. The presence of her mother (far left) was very important, not only for Pearl but also for the children who needed reassurance and a sense of continuity.

existence with John, but she was not drowning. She may have received a terrible blow but her instinct was to struggle to her feet again. Her diary shows that even when she was in a state of shock, she was nevertheless very aware of the feelings of others, even on the day that John died –

> *Poor dear Rachel – my darling was her only near member of the family left … Mummy came round and I wanted to break it to her gently because of her heart. One is so stunned.*
> (30 MARCH)

As the news of John's death became known, the letters flooded in, *'such wonderful letters'* –

> *Those I prize are those from his old men friends and oh! how they loved him and the 'would be' official letters from his Boards and Societies who poured out their heartfelt regret at their loss.* (5 APRIL)

These letters must have given Pearl an insight into other parts of John's life that she – a whole generation younger than her husband – could never have shared. They also provided a reflection of how he was valued in a much wider sphere. His loss was far more than a personal and local one as Charles Greenway, one of the founders of the Anglo-Persian Oil Company, observed to Pearl –

> *I have long been an admirer of your late husband as being one of the few peers who do an honour to their country in the part they take in public work and devotion to their fellow men. The loss is not yours only but a national one!* (2 APRIL 1929)

A recurring theme was the enduring affection and respect that he had inspired. One such letter came from Charles St John Hornby, an old friend from John's Oxford days. He summed up very movingly the quality and strength of a friendship first made more than 40 years earlier –

> *John was almost my oldest Oxford friend. From those early days I had a very great affection for him, and although in after years our paths lay apart and we did not often see one another, that affection never changed, and when we did meet we met as though we had never parted. Of all the men I have known I think he was the most lovable, full of that charm which you cannot describe in words but which no one who knew him could fail to feel the spell of. And over and above that he was a man of great gifts, which he used in a multitude of ways in the service of others.*

I have lost this last year my two best Oxford friends, John and Freddie Smith, both of them in their different ways, the best of men. They were stroke and 7 of the first New College VIII I rowed in, in 1888. I shall never forget those days and the glamour of our friendship. No friends made in after years are ever the same, or nearly the same.
(3 APRIL 1929)

Another aspect of John's life was reflected in a letter from the wife of Arthur Jacomb. Arthur had been the engine driver when Pearl and John travelled by train to Beaulieu on their wedding day and Mrs Jacomb recalled an early phase in John's career –

Such a Dear Friend to Mr Jacomb and his Railway Companion. And I Cannot refrain from saying they will always value His True kindness of Heart. Also his worth. And strange to say that, when His Lordship was a young gentleman apprentice at Nine Elms my own Father then an Engine Driver, gave His Lordship his first ride on the footplate.
(4 APRIL 1929)

If John's friends were shocked and saddened by his death, the effect on all those at Beaulieu was profound indeed. John had embodied the spirit of the place with his energy and the strength of his personality, as one friend wrote to Pearl –

It seems hardly possible to believe that the sunshine and joyous spirit that radiated from the Palace and permeated the atmosphere of Beaulieu with a sense of happiness and youthful cheer has become dimmed and the soul of the people touched with sadness. (10 APRIL 1929)

There is evidence from the surviving letters of a deep sense of destabilisation amongst the tenants – a feeling of bewilderment and, inevitably, uncertainty about the future. Mrs Malcom of Clobb Farm expressed this most graphically in an undated letter, using a phrase that must have resonated with Pearl –

May God give you strength to bear up for your little children's sake and I also feel that when you are brave, it is a comfort to your Dear Departed. We as his tenants feel like the sheep without the Shepherd. May God guide and comfort you in your sorrow.

Similarly, Frank Wadley, 'the great Frank Wadley', as Captain Widnell described him, and the Estate's electrical engineer, echoed this thought when he wrote –

> *I have lost a Loving Chief, and my heart goes out to you in your great trial.*
> (31 MARCH 1929)

More than most, Frank Wadley was in a position to understand something of what Pearl was going through – his second wife had died in the influenza pandemic of 1918 leaving him with three young children.

John Mills at Bisterne, who was one of the trustees for the Estate, testified not only to John's personal qualities, but also to the happiness that he had found in his marriage to Pearl –

My dear Pearl,

We are absolutely horrified, Carola and I, at this awful news. We have been so dreading a tragedy for you that we just didn't dare think of it – and its all the harder to believe that it can be true and that John with his intense vitality and perpetual youth has gone from us all. Those two characteristics and his wonderful charm made him irresistible as a friend; his almost boyish enthusiasm and his real wisdom and breadth of view were so intriguing and inspiring and it seems almost too wonderful that he should have honoured my duller mind with his friendship. The loss of him is a national one.

We heard on the wireless last night and Carola could hardly sleep for thinking of you – with this at the end of your long, long anxiety. But in Church this morning I did hope that when my turn to go came, it might be near Easter, so that I, like John, could leave behind me for those I loved the message that the parting was not for ever – but that some day, some where, some how, we'd meet again.

I think it must be given to few women to give their husbands such wonderful happiness as you have given John in these years – such perfect companionship and then his whole life's longing of a son. (31 MARCH 1929)

This last sentiment was echoed by another correspondent –

I shall always remember when we met again after his marriage to you, the joy and pride with which he spoke of you and your beauty, and his great happiness in having met you. In these days of half-hearted marriages it was wonderful to see his love for you.

The Duke of Buccleuch wrote to Pearl on 10 April, his letter brief and to the point –

You can anyhow console yourself with the thought that you gave him several years of great happiness. Harry Forster will be a great help to you. I know no one who is more level headed or can give better advice.

A litter collection exercise in the New Forest in 1931. Pearl had to take on John's role in the local community as well as managing the estate and bringing up her young children. On 29 December 1929 she wrote after seeing a family film John had taken the previous year, *I realise how thin I have got when I see what a fat face I had.*

'The tragedy of it all'

Pearl was in need of good advice, particularly since the entire structure of her life was being recast at a time of general economic uncertainty. John's death, 24 years after that of his father, meant that the Beaulieu Estate was, for the second time, assessed for death duties. Although inheritance tax in the form of legacy, succession and estate duties had been levied since 1796, the introduction of death duties in 1894 at a top rate of eight per cent hit the larger estates much harder. By 1920 the rate was 30 per cent. The reality of the financial position had to be addressed immediately and here Harry Forster's help was invaluable –

> *Harry sat on and read out bits of the Will to me and discussed plans. Oh! the decisions and oh! the cruelty of Death and Succession Duties! We want to try and let Palace House for a summer let and then later let it for 7 years. The tragedy of it all.*
> (5 APRIL)

Pearl's diary entries for in the immediate aftermath of John's death describe how she was able to maintain a form of equilibrium by focusing on what had to be done, and somehow steering a course through what must have felt like uncharted water. As in the days following the death of Harry Cubitt, it seems that her diary provided an outlet for feelings that might otherwise have been hard to express to others. In John's absence, Pearl had become a figurehead, not only for her immediately family but also for Beaulieu and, as she well knew, that figurehead had to be seen to be strong. Pearl's diary shows how that the presence of Clara and the Forsters was a lifeline for her in those first painful days –

> *Another glorious day. Stayed in bed till after lunch and then we all went down to Lepe and took the children too. Harry, Mummy and Rachel and I walked about the gardens and the children went on the Shore for a bit. Never have I seen a more perfect day. We all had tea there. It seemed so awful looking up my darling's river and all over the Solent on which we'd been so much together – my sorrow comes over me so crashingly at times.*
> (6 APRIL)

> *Rachel, Harry and I went to church at 8. Afterwards we went across to look at the lovely wreaths on my darling's grave. In spite of 7 degrees of frost they are still lovely. Such a glorious morning. Had Edward and Caroline down to breakfast. I didn't go to 11 service but Capt Widnell and I had a long talk walking up and down in front of the house in the sun – it is the first time I have seen him since and I longed for him and others to*

realise how much I appreciated everything that was done and how much I hoped that he and Ashmead would 'stay on' and help the Trustees and me. We have such a huge responsibility and pray God I shall be given strength not to fail and do as he would have wished. Ted Crispin and Tommie came in after church re shooting to see Harry and me. Saw Tubbie Clayton and Nellie SW after church. Rested between 3 and 4 and then decided not to get up again. Dear Harry went off to Southampton and caught the 4.45. He goes back to Pau tomorrow. I feel so glad. He had been quite too wonderful to me all through these last weeks and days. He is such a rock of strength and so sound and gentle. (7 APRIL)

Captain Widnell had offered his resignation to Pearl, but this had not been accepted. The people who were to ensure that the Estate survived intact were taking up their places, even in the first confused weeks after John's death.

Some decisions were very clear-cut, based as much on sentiment as on economy, including the decision to sell the Rolls-Royce –

I couldn't bear even to see her again. Oh! the miles of happy touring we have done together in her! …. we discussed selling Cygnet [John's motor boat] *as well.* (5 APRIL)

The following weeks were intensely busy for Pearl in starting the process of settling John's professional and personal affairs as well as taking up the reins of the Estate –

Got up before breakfast – as had such a lot to do. Jack Mills came over to lunch to advise me re price to let the sea trout fishing. After lunch Tommie T, Jack Mills, Mr Ashmead and I went up above Hartford Hole to show Jack the river and then we walked down to Black Bridge and so back by car to the stables – from there we walked across the Park to show him the work done to Boarman's Pond and ask his advice for letting the fishing on it. It was so kind and helpful. Felt busy and keen while out – but suddenly very lonely and missy when I got back. (10 APRIL)

Went to Lymington and tried on black coat and skirt and saw Drew about photos of my darling which I want to give to Palace House staff and all the 74 watchers round his dear body while in church and all his devoted heads in each department. Called to see old Robbins at Hatchett and he chose a photo – then to Hilda and Wadley and Ashmead and then on to see Wadley at his house – we wept together – and had a long talk. Oh! how they adored my darling 'his devoted Chief for 35 years!' Then Kitcher came to see me at 12.30 – and he and I did the same. Poor old Davis is quite broken – no one in Beaulieu felt that my darling wouldn't come back – it was such a dreadful shock to all his 'friends' as he called every one. With the help of his devoted staff I hope to 'carry on' as he would have wished. At 1.45 Mummy came with me to Winchester where I had to go and see Miss Porter re the AA19 number off the Rolls as it was my darling's old number and he paid £5.0.0 to retain it. They have allocated a new number for the Rolls to send it to Mr Pedley. (11 APRIL)

A few days at Hindhead with Gladys, where Anne and Nooie had been staying, provided some respite. Brief references in the diary hint at the extent of the physical and mental strain that Pearl was experiencing –

Staying with Gladie Wheelside, Hindhead. Spent a lazy morning then after lunch Gladie and I went for a walk for exercise …. Little Anne is so sweet – Nooie was so wonderful the way she told her about her darling Daddy – it was so wonderful him 'passing over' on Easter Saturday with all the beauty of the thoughts of the Resurrection which made it easier to tell the little thing. She is the only one of our little 4 who will really remember their Daddy. It is all so tragic. (13 APRIL)

Nooie and I went to church at 8 at St Albans, Hindhead, Service beautifully taken. Gladie kindly sent up in her car …. Gladie and I spent a peaceful day, writing letters in the garden and then had a nice walk. Feeling better – at least find I want food more. We counted that up to date I have had 563 letters – all of which I love. (14 APRIL)

A glorious day. … Sat out in the summer house till 12.15 …. Darling Nooie washed my hair after tea. When did she wash it last? Probably in 1909 at St Leonards! (15 APRIL)

Very exhausted – I find everything such a mental strain. Had a long talk on telephone to Mummy and Rachel re an American who came over Palace House yesterday and want to take it – they seemed nice types. (16 APRIL)

Anne and Caroline help with seine fishing (drag netting) the Beaulieu River in 1931. Pearl had seen this time-honoured method of fishing on her first visit to Beaulieu in June 1920 when John was still 'Lord Montagu' to her.

The return home signalled a very busy phase of sorting and organising – a painful and wearying task – as well as catching up with friends and people on the estate. There was also John's London office to dismantle. (Jane Clowes had been John's secretary.) All this was being done scarcely a month after his death –

> It has done me such a lot of good and I want my food again though I am not digesting it very well. Teddie arrived in Helen's car at 12 and after lunch we started back and arrived home at 4.20 to be greeted on the doorstep by Mummy and all the little family …. Probate people, Mr Lofts, were waiting for me to help them do the silver and to show what was mine – not to value – so worked with …. Jane came to stay. (18 APRIL)

> Mr Lofts and his probate men are here from 9.30 continuing the silver and we did my darling's little pieces of jewellery and then Tommie came down and I went through all the pictures with the special picture man. That took all the morning. I went off at 9.45 and fetched my two boxes of jewellery out of the Bank. Found little silver of any value in the silver room (by that I mean old silver – which is lucky). They were finished by 1.15. The three pieces they like best are our 3 screens. (19 APRIL)

> One hour short last night and Rachel and I went to church at 8 and after had a long talk to the Vicar and then went on to my darling's grave and tidied up. Such a beautiful day. I wrote letters in our outdoor room till after church when Nellie Ryder came to see me – I hadn't seen her to talk to since. She is so sweet. I opened the gardens to Beaulieu people to see the daffs today – they did so love it – talked to Mrs Norris. All say the same that we are stunned, we cannot believe that my beloved darling has gone for ever. It is so wonderful for me to realise how tremendously he was loved by all. (21 APRIL)

> Had a very trying morning. Rachel helped me turn out 2 of my darling's writing table drawers and also box full of private papers and letters which we burnt. I kept a few nice old letters from John to his father and Rachel kept some of her brother Robert's. After lunch I went on sorting and dividing up my darling's clothes. So very very harrowing. (24 APRIL)

Spent the morning going through my darling's clothes again. At 11 the Vicar, Rachel and I met Mr Hayson in the Burial Ground to see drawings and a pattern carving on the Hopton Wood stone for the slab which the Vicar is giving on which are the words of the 16th century Prayer which my darling asked to be put near his grave. (25 APRIL)

4 weeks today at 10.10 my very dearly beloved 'passed away' at 29 Wimpole Str .... I am trying so hard to be brave – as he would wish. Everyone here says the same – his spirit is everywhere in Beaulieu. Everyone expects to see him any moment, anywhere. We talk about him all day long and I want Beaulieu to talk about him and then we shall never lose his atmosphere for little Edward's sake. I stayed in bed today – very busy with Gravestock going through all the jewellery. Darling Rachel went back to Lepe today after having been here with me just a month – she has been such a joy to me and such a help with all the turning out. (27 APRIL)

Left Beaulieu at 8.20 and caught 8.41 Beaulieu Road .... to Jane at 62 where we did things together. Each day she goes through the files and destroys a lot but oh! what cruel work. Really Jane's life has been wrapped up in her work in the office with my beloved as her devoted Chief – and all his especially kept files have to be gone through and so much Car Illustrated stuff too .... Then Jane and I went to Nicholsons [John's tailor] *and saw all his uniforms and Peers robe.* (1 MAY)

There was also estate business to be attended to, and the search for possible tenants for Palace House. Pearl had to face the upheaval of letting her own home –

Went to see Jane at the office on my way to Nichol Manisty, 1 Howard St where Tommie T and I, Widdie and Ashmead met (the three came up from Beaulieu by early train) and Mr Nichol tried to explain to us and answer many questions! Were there till 1.10. Rachel F, Jane and I lunched with Aunt Netty and then Tommie T, Brockleby and I met at 62 for the Clitheroe Board meeting. Geoffrey Marks arrived at 3 and we elected him Director and Chairman in place of my beloved. All very wearying for me – reading all my darling's notes at the last Clitheroe Board Meeting .... Widdie and Ashmead came in and we telephoned to several agents re letting Palace House. (2 MAY)

Absolutely deluging. Jane and I had a morning of turning out my darling's writing table drawers. Found his little diary of 1920 and found on May 9th he had put 'Kensington

Gardens, God's Gift'!!! That was me! The day we became engaged! Then I found the original rough copy of the beautiful little poem he wrote me and sent me on our wedding day, Aug 10th 1920. All so wonderful for me – but oh! how agonising! Laura and Tommie lunched …. Still went on turning out till tea time when Rachel brought Miss Carlton and a Mrs Warns from South Australia over from Lepe – showed her round the house and then she took her round Abbey. Still raining. After dinner Mummy and Jane helped me turn out an old case – found treasures of his father and his Oxford days and railway 'shop' days – all so interesting. (5 MAY)

Busy writing till lunch. When Jack and Carola Mills came over – he especially to help me go into the wine cellar and see what my darling had and list it. We spent about ¾ hour at it and he is going to advise me about it. …. I felt so terribly depressed as I always do after a heavy job on hand and when it is over – such awful reaction sets in. I felt I must have a walk so they took me in the car and dropped me a bit across the heath from Hatchett. I met Smith the forest keeper and had a long talk about my darling – he said they missed him so at the Verderers court yesterday. (7 MAY)

Raining slightly – Geoffrey Marks (one of my Executors) helped me sign the form for the cheque of the Scottish Widow's Life Policy on my darling's life – and then he and I and Tommie T went up to the Manor office, there joined by Jack Mills from Bisterne and with Capt Widnell and Ashmead we showed them the workings of the Estate – possible sales of land, or houses on a 99 years lease! (11 MAY)

But all the busyness couldn't stop the memories – the fine weather at Whitsun reminding Pearl of one particular time just before the birth of Mary Clare the previous year –

The most perfect day, still and warm although Whitsun last year was a fortnight later. My beloved and I had the most perfect honeymoon here alone together. We were out on the sea all day, Saturday, Sunday and Tuesday. Oh! how I miss our sea life. I couldn't bear to go in Cygnet again – but to go out on the sea! (19 MAY)

Pearl and the children at Beaulieu amongst the springtime daffodils in April 1934. Idyllic as it looks, Pearl records the next day that Edward had started a cold and Anne had gone into the Lymington Cottage Hospital to have her tonsils removed.

The most perfect day. Still and hot. Capt Holder rang up and asked me and anyone else to go on his motor boat this afternoon which will be lovely and so kind …. Everything seems so unreal! Beaulieu River and the Solent without John! (20 MAY)

'My anchor of life has gone'

As the weeks rolled on, Pearl became more involved in social events and revisiting the places she had known with John. Very movingly, she used a yachting metaphor to describe the enormity of her loss and its destabilising effect. The years with John had given her a sense of continuity and safety which had now disappeared –

Another perfect morning. At 10.15 we all started off in two cars to Lymington Yacht Club where we met Major & Mrs Matthews – they have been lent the Henry Monds chartered ketch, 115 tons Gwendoline while they are electioneering at Liverpool – so invited us all out. We went out a good way into the Solent where we boarded her. No breeze – so went under engine and jib till off Ryde went on turning – we could just keep steady against tide and wind – off Cowes we picked up a nice breeze and had a good sail back. Quite lovely – but oh! the Solent without my darling – and looking at Cowes and the Squadron, it seems so unreal. I have hardly ever been out except with my beloved. We got back at 7. A perfect day and must have done us all good. Very lonely and depressed this evening – my anchor of life has gone – I haven't even a kedge so far. (26 MAY)

I feel suddenly (after 8 years of complete security) so unprotected! Such an odd feeling. (27 MAY)

The yearning for John showed itself in the desire to maintain the connection with those who had cared for him in his final illness. During a trip to London that summer, Pearl paid a visit to the nursing home where he had died –

My beloved's birthday today. 9 years ago since I gave him his first present (the note case which he used till the day he died) …. When I was at Debenhams – so near Wimpole Str – I felt I must go and see Miss Lankaster at No 29 – so bought her some flowers and again walked down Wimpole St – rang the bell as I did every day for 6 weeks. Oh! the memories. Found dear Miss Lankaster so pleased to see me – we had a nice talk – then Nurse Shaw came down to see me – Miss Lankaster hopes to come and stay on Saturday 29th – I so want her to know Beaulieu – as she was so sweet to John. (10 JUNE)

Meanwhile tenants were found for Palace House and Pearl and the family went to the House on the Shore –

> *Fearfully busy finishing up at locking up in Palace House – it is a job getting out of Palace House – only for a few weeks – one just dreads to think what it will be when we let for a term of years! Jane came and helped and lunched …. I hate leaving Beaulieu, if only for a bit and of course going to the House on the Shore brings back all the memories of the moves there with John just this time last year.* (31 JULY)

The business of settling John's estate continued –

> *At 2.30 I was at 1 Bedford Row to see Mr Rowcliffe about my Will and then at 3.45 with Charles Nicholl to hear again all about the probate papers etc. I left there at 6.30 – I was 3½ hours with lawyers!!* (24 SEPTEMBER)

On 30 September Pearl commented –

> *Six whole months today since my own beloved left me and Beaulieu and all those he loved. Feel very missy. It isn't getting any easier.*

As time went on Pearl found some consolation although this was precariously balanced with an all-pervading sense of profound loss. She was still visiting places last seen with John –

> *Tommie T and Vin came round in my car to fetch me at 9.45 and we joined the guns of the syndicate at St Leonards. …. I have never been out shooting here without my darling – all too strange – I wore his mac all day and felt a warm glowy feeling, he was near me all the time – it was lovely. But the woods without John – oh! every inch of the way was John to me.* (23 NOVEMBER)

> *Anne and I had such a lovely walk down Summer Lane and right along the bank in front of Buckler's Hard. The last time Anne and I came with my darling and Anne remembers every word he said – it is so lovely for me to feel I have one little kiddie who remembers and loves her Daddy as he was – his thoughts and words.* (24 NOVEMBER)

Clara spent Christmas 1929 at Beaulieu together with Gladys and Cyril and their children. The day after, Rachel Forster wrote to Pearl –

> *I have been thinking of you so much at this Christmastide and wishing I could help and comfort you – for I know how much you must have missed him – and how gallantly you have tried to make things brighter for everyone. You are really splendid in your unselfishness and I am sure he is watching you and feeling so proud of you – even more than he always did when he was so visibly with you and that is saying a great deal. How he loved you darling and how happy you made him. That is always something to be ever glad and proud of.*

On 29 March 1930, Pearl wrote – *I can't think how I can have lived a whole year without my darling John.* That summer Palace House was again let, a necessary financial move but a stressful task for Pearl with four young children to accommodate. She made the very best of the situation but in some ways it must have felt like a replay of her own peripatetic childhood.

There was a long road ahead of Pearl – that meeting with John in 1920 had changed her life and set her on a course that she was to follow for more than 70 years. The love and commitment that John had felt for Beaulieu, and the love and commitment that Pearl had for John became fused. From now on, Pearl had two chief aims – to bring up her family as John would have wished, and to do all that she could for the place that John had once described as 'his little Kingdom'. A chance discovery a few months after his death seemed to clarify this for her –

> *I looked in a Beaulieu Abbey book in my boudoir (a room which makes me so sad now as I have not used it since my happy days before my darling and I went to London on Feb 18th) and found 'To Pearl from John, hoping that she will love the Abbey as much as he does.' I had quite forgotten that he had written like that! I do love the Abbey with a passion and my great desire will be to bring up his kiddies to love it as he did.* (9 JULY)

Anne (seated centre, Caroline (standing left), Edward and Mary Clare photographed at Beaulieu in 1936. Edward had succeeded to the title of Baron Montagu of Beaulieu at the age of 2½.

WHO'S WHO OF THE DIARY

♦♦♦

Pearl habitually recorded the names of the people she encountered, whether those she met only once or people she saw regularly and who made up her daily life. Some of these individuals are well documented while others, such as Nanny Champ who played a key role in the lives of the young Montagus, have remained so elusive that only the barest details can be given.

ANSTRUTHER The Honourable Dame Eva (1869-1935)

Eva Anstruther was an old friend of John's and lived in Beaulieu. Her daughter Joyce (1901-1953) who wrote under the name of Jan Struther, created the character of Mrs Miniver, originally for a column in *The Times* in the 1930s. During the Second World War *Mrs Miniver* was made into a highly successful book and film. Pearl eventually read the book at the age of 95.

BELL Gertrude Margaret Lowthian (1868-1926)

Traveller, writer and archaeologist, Gertrude Bell was a significant figure in the politics of the Middle East, having been employed in army intelligence by the British government in the First World War. Pearl and John saw Gertrude at Crathorne in 1923 when Gertrude and her father, Sir Hugh Bell, came to lunch, noting on 19 August, *John was so interested to meet Miss Bell – she returns to Baghdad on Wednesday on Government job. She had not been home for 4 years when she came back on leave in May.* Gertrude died unexpectedly in Baghdad at the age of 57.

BELL Sir Hugh (1844-1931)

Sir Hugh and his family were friends and close neighbours of Lionel and Violet Dugdale in Yorkshire. A ball given at the Bell family home, Rounton Grange, in December 1912 had a special significance for Pearl as she was embarking on her debutante year – she described it as 'really my first dance'. When Sir Hugh heard that Pearl was visiting the Middle East in 1927, he asked her help in making arrangements for marking Gertrude's grave.

BUCCLEUCH John Charles, 7th Duke of (1864-1935)

The first cousin of John Montagu, he married Lady Margaret Bridgeman, daughter of 4th Earl of Bradford, and had eight children. One daughter married Prince Henry, Duke of Gloucester becoming Princess Alice, Duchess of Gloucester.

BURTON Decimus (1800-1881)

Architect and garden designer and son of the developer James Burton, Decimus was responsible for a large number of buildings in the seaside resort of St Leonards in East Sussex in the 1850s. Amongst the many other buildings he designed is the Athenaeum Club in Pall Mall, London – both both he and his father were founder members.

CHAMP

Remembered affectionately by the Montagu family as a portly cockney, Nannie Champ was recruited by Pearl to look after all her children as babies and toddlers.

CLAYTON Reverend Philip Thomas Byard 'Tubbie' (1885-1972)

A First World War chaplain on the Western Front, Tubbie Clayton was the founder of the international Christian movement 'Toc H' (Talbot House). A friend of John Montagu, he took John's funeral service together with the Reverend Powles. There is a memorial to him in Beaulieu Abbey Church.

CLOWES Alice Maud 'Jane' 1881-1948

Jane Clowes was John Montagu's secretary, a role that became more important after the death of his personal assistant Eleanor Thornton in 1915. Jane relocated from London to Beaulieu in 1926 and remained with the family after John died in 1929. Her work in helping to sort out John's affairs was invaluable to Pearl, who evidently regarded her more as a friend and companion than an employee. On 1 May 1929, a month after John's death, Pearl wrote, *Each day she* [Jane] *goes through the files and destroys a lot but oh! what cruel work.*

CRAKE Clara Alice *née* Woodroffe (1868-1954)

Pearl's mother. *See* Chapter 1.

CRAKE Dorothy Barrington (1883-1962)

Twin sister of Winifred Crake and Pearl's half-sister, Dorothy married Colonel Reginald (Reggie) Edmund Maghlin Russell (1879-1950) in Egypt in 1918. Russell had a wide-ranging military career including service in South Africa, Egypt, Sudan and South America as well as a spell in the newly formed RAF between 1918 and 1920 where he served as a pilot.

CRAKE Major Edward Barrington (1854-1910)

Pearl's father. *See* Chapter 1.

CRAKE Gladys Louisa Violet (1896-1977)

Pearl's full sister, Gladys married Major Cubitt (*see* Cubitt, Charles) on 10 November 1919. He and Gladys had five sons. Pearl and Gladys remained close companions and allies as adults. On 12 October 1977, the day that Gladys died, Pearl wrote in her diary that she and her beloved sister 'were everything to each other.'

CRAKE Vandeleur Benjamin (1816-1894)

Pearl's paternal grandfather. *See* Chapter 1.

CRAKE William (1787-1863)

Pearl's paternal great-grandfather. *See* Chapter 1.

CRAKE Winifred Dorothy (1883-1969)

Pearl's half-sister and twin daughter of Edward Crake by his first wife, Caroline Follett, Winifred married Captain Josslyn Seymour Egerton (1893-c.1946) of the Coldstream Guards in 1913.

CROUCH John (1867-1923)

A boyhood friend of John Montagu born and brought up on the Beaulieu Estate, John Crouch became his gamekeeper at the age of 19. The two men, who were almost the same age, had a deep affection for each other. Pearl described her husband as 'terribly grieved' when John Crouch died, noting that his death might have been avoidable if medical assistance had been called in earlier.

CUBITT Lieutenant Alick George (Hussars) (1894-1917)

The second son of Henry and Maud Cubitt, Alick was killed on 24 November 1917 on the Western Front. Pearl was staying at Denbies, the Cubitt family home, when the news was received, writing in her diary on 27 November, *One feels too numb to think. It is all too ghastly!*

CUBITT Major Charles Cyril (Grenadier Guards) (1896-1971)

Major Cubitt, always known as Cyril, was descended from Lewis Cubitt, a brother of the builder, Thomas Cubitt, and so was a distant cousin of Harry Cubitt. He was wounded twice in the First World War. *See* Crake, Gladys

CUBITT Henry, 2nd Baron Ashcombe (1867-1947)

Henry succeeded to the baronetcy in 1917. He and his wife, Maud (1865-1945), became close friends of Pearl after Harry's death. Henry signed the register as one of the witnesses at Pearl and John's wedding, while Maud became a godmother to their first child, Anne. Pearl referred to them as 'Cousin Henry' and 'Cousin Maud'.

CUBITT Captain Henry 'Harry' Archibald (Coldstream Guards) (1892-1916)

The eldest son of Henry (later 2nd Baron Ashcombe) and his wife Maud, Harry became informally engaged to Pearl in 1916. *See* Chapter 3.

CUBITT Lieutenant Roland Calvert (Coldstream Guards) (1899-1962)

The fourth of the six sons of Henry and Maud Cubitt, Roland married Sonia Keppel (1900-1986) the daughter of Lt-Col. the Hon. George Keppel and his wife, Alice. As the eldest surviving son, Roland became 3rd Baron Ashcombe in 1947.

CUBITT Lieutenant William Hugh (1st Royal Dragoons) (1896-1918)

The third son of Henry and Maud Cubitt and always known as Hugh, Lieutenant Cubitt was killed in France on 24 March 1918. He received his commission in November 1914 and was sent to the Western Front in May 1915, serving there continuously with the Cavalry Corps. On hearing the news on 2 April, Pearl wrote – *3 precious sons in 18 months gone. Feel absolutely distraught.*

DOUGLAS-SCOTT-MONTAGU

(See Montagu*)*

DUGDALE Beryl Violet (1902-1994)

The only daughter of Lionel and Violet Dugdale, Beryl married Malcolm George Dyer-Edwardes Leslie (1902-1975) later 20th Earl of Rothes in 1926. On hearing the news of their engagement on 18 March 1926 Pearl wrote – *We met him at Crathorne and thought him so charming – he has been in love for ages but has very little money and now his Godfather Mr O'Dwyer Edmonds has just died and makes it possible, they have known each other for two years. So pleased.*

DUGDALE Captain James Lionel (1862–1941)

Lionel Dugdale was responsible for the construction of a magnificent country house, Crathorne Hall, near Yarm in Yorkshire. Now a hotel, Crathorne was effectively a second home for Pearl and her sister Gladys and the scene of many a happy gathering for friends and family.

DUGDALE Maud Violet *née* Crake (1873–1940)

The youngest sister of Clara Crake, and Pearl's 'Aunt Vi', Violet married Lionel Dugdale in 1894. *See* Chapter 2.

DUGDALE Thomas 'Tom' Lionel (1897–1977)

Tom was the only son of Lionel and Violet Dugdale and 1st Baron Crathorne from 1959. Educated at Eton and Sandhurst, he later became a Conservative MP and chairman of the party. He married Nancy Tennant in 1936.

EGERTON Captain Josslyn 'Joss' Seymour (Coldstream Guards) (1893–1946)

See Crake, Winifred.

FORSTER Rachel Cecily, *née* Douglas-Scott-Montagu (1868–1962), and Henry 'Harry' William, 1st Baron Forster of Lepe (1866–1936).

John Montagu's sister, Rachel, married Henry Forster in 1890. A Conservative politician, Henry was created 1st Baron Forster of Lepe in 1919 and, in 1920, appointed Governor-General of Australia where he and Rachel stayed for five years. Both of their sons were killed in the First World War. The Forsters' support was essential to Pearl following John's death.

FOWLER Sir James Kingston (1852–1934)

A distinguished physician and keen amateur historian, Sir James was an old friend of John Montagu, who asked him to write a history of Beaulieu Abbey. He built a house called 'The Vineyards' at Beaulieu.

GLYN Juliet (1898–1964)

Juliet was the younger daughter of Elinor Glyn (1854–1943), a successful romantic novelist. She and her sister, Margot (1893–1966), are mentioned as part of a group of friends in the South of France when Pearl's visit there in 1914. Juliet featured several times in subsequent diaries and was one of Pearl's bridesmaids. In 1921 she married Sir Rhys Rhys-Williams, a Liberal politician more than twice her age. She later became a governor of the BBC.

GREENWAY Sir Charles (1857–1934)

One of the founders of the Anglo-Persian Oil Company (APOC) and an old friend of John Montagu, Charles Greenway was responsible for making the arrangements for John and Pearl's extensive tour of the Middle East in 1927.

HELY-HUTCHINSON Melita Agnes Mary, *née* Keppel (1892-1987)

Melita and her sister Maria (1891-1976) were distant cousins of Pearl. As girls they lived in London where their father Admiral Colin Keppel was an equery to Edward VII and George V. Melita and Maria were guests at Pearl's coming-out ball in 1912. Melita married Maurice Hely-Hutchinson (1887-1961) in 1920. Marie married the 6th Earl of Romney in 1918.

KEPPEL Henrietta Mary, *née* Blundell-Hollinshead-Blundell (1868-1957)

Referred to as 'Cousin Etta' in the diary, Henrietta was distantly related to Pearl through the Woodroffes. She married Admiral Colin Keppel in 1889. *See* Hely-Hutchinson, Melita.

LEWIN Beatrice Emily 'Queenie', *née* Barlow Webb (1883-1969)

Queenie was the sister of Sissie Woodroffe (*see* Woodroffe, Eleanor). She married Captain Charles McLean Lewin (1880-1919) of the 4th Queen's Own Hussars in 1908. Leila Dorothy Barlow Webb (1889-1978) was the youngest of the three sisters.

LUMLEY Second Lieutenant Richard 'Dick' John (11th Prince Albert's Own Hussars) (1894-1914)

Dick Lumley's name crops up frequently in Pearl's diaries between 1912 and 1914. He was one of the guests at the Crathorne house party for Pearl's coming out ball in 1912 and he evidently formed part of a close group of friends. His death so early in the War gave Pearl her first direct experience of loss within her own circle.

MATURIN Dr Francis Henry, Lieutenant Colonel TD (1871-1939)

Local doctor based in Lymington, Hampshire, who delivered Pearl's second, still-born child, the only one of her babies to be born at Beaulieu.

MILLS Major John Digby (1879-1972)

John Mills and his wife, Carola, were old friends of John Montagu and lived at Bisterne Manor some 20 miles west of Beaulieu. Major Mills was one of the trustees of John's estate.

MONTAGU Anne Rachel Pearl (1921-2015)

Pearl and John's eldest daughter. *See* Chapter 6.

MONTAGU Caroline Cecily (born 1925)

Pearl and John's second daughter. *See* Chapter 6.

MONTAGU Cecil Victoria Constance, *née* Kerr Baroness Montagu of Beaulieu (1866-1919)

John Montagu's first wife, Cecil (Cis) died of complications following Spanish Influenza. The two were first cousins, Cis's mother being John's Aunt Victoria (1844-1938) who had married Schomberg Kerr, 9th Marquis of Lothian (1833-1900).

MONTAGU Edward John Barrington, 3rd Baron Montagu of Beaulieu (1926-2015)

Pearl and John's only son. *See* Chapter 6.

MONTAGU Elizabeth Susan (1909-2002)

John Montagu's younger daughter by his first wife. *See* Chapter 5.

MONTAGU Helen Cecil (1890-1969)

John Montagu's elder daughter by his first wife. *See* Chapter 5.

MONTAGU Henry John, 1st Baron Montagu of Beaulieu (1832-1905)

Father of John Montagu, Henry was responsible for the rebuilding of Palace House in its present form in the early 1870s. He was created 1st Baron Montagu in 1885.

MONTAGU Brigadier-General John Walter Edward, 2nd Baron Montagu of Beaulieu (1866-1929)

See Chapter 4.

MONTAGU Mary Clare (1928-2016)

Pearl and John's third daughter. *See* Chapter 6.

PLUMER Field Marshall Herbert Charles Onslow, 1st Viscount Plumer (1857-1932)

Plumer had commanded the Second Army on the Western Front between 1915 and 1917, winning an outstanding victory at the Battle of Messines in 1917 with the deployment of underground mines. Appointed High Commissioner of the British Mandate for Palestine in 1925, he remained firm in the face of requests by Arab nationalists to cancel undertakings made in the Balfour Declaration. He and his wife were Pearl and John's hosts in Jerusalem in 1927.

POWLES The Reverend Robert Frazer (1846-1942)

After ordination, Rev Powles served a curacy at Christchurch, St Leonards, before becoming a curate at Beaulieu in 1880. Six years later he took over the living remaining there until his resignation in 1939 due to ill health. He exerted a powerful influence in the parish. Captain Widnell described him as *a revered and deeply loved dictator, both in the church, and indeed on the estate, as far as he was able.* He officiated at Pearl and John's marriage in 1920.

RUSSELL Colonel Reginald 'Reggie' Edmund Maghlin (1879-1950)

See Crake, Dorothy Barrington

STEPHENS 'Teddy'

Teddy was John Montagu's chauffeur and was probably accompanying John when he first met Pearl in 1920. Captain Widnell described Teddy as *in some ways the ideal chauffeur, one of his great virtues being that he remembered every single bag and piece of luggage aboard his car, so that before re-starting after any stop, long or short, Teddy, if his eagle eye should miss anything, would not fail to ask his chief, 'Have you got your little brown bag, or walking stick?' or whatever it might have been.*

THORNTON Eleanor Velasco (1880-1915)

Personal assistant and mistress to John Montagu by whom she had a daughter, Eleanor was the model for the face of the figure of the 'Spirit of Ecstasy' that adorns the bonnet of Rolls Royce cars. She died when the SS *Persia* was torpedoed in 1915 as she and John were on their way to India. John survived thanks to his Gieves inflatable waistcoat. *See* Clowes, Jane

TOWNSHEND Henrietta (1850-1950) and Janet (1845-1922)

Henrietta, referred to in the diary as 'Aunt Netty' and her sister Janet were collectively known as 'the Aunts'. They were the sisters of Pearl's maternal grandmother, Alice Crake, and both were an important presence in Pearl's life. When Janet died on 21 October 1922 Pearl recorded, *Poor Aunt Netty, one dreads to think of her life without Aunt Janet —they have lived together for 70 years and have been just all to each other.* The death of Henrietta on 27 November 1950 meant the end of an era for Pearl who wrote in her diary — *So ends the perfect life of the sweetest person aged 100 years 8 months who has been loved by 4 generations of her devoted family — all ages adore her. A quite unique person in our small family of nephews, nieces, greats, great greats, and great great greats.*

TOWNSHEND Henry Leigh (1842–1924)

The brother of Henrietta, Janet and Alice Townshend (*see* Woodroffe, Alice), Henry was known in the family as 'Uncle Harry'. A self-made millionaire who had bought and rebuilt Caldecote Hall in Warwickshire, he died in 1924 in a drowning accident at Caldecote. When Pearl heard the news on 1 May that year she wrote, *He was a splendid old man of 82 – but so hale and hearty.*

TROUBRIDGE Sir Thomas 'Tommie' Herbert Cochrane (Baronet) (1860–1938)

One of John Montagu's greatest friends, Tommie built a house, Oldways, at the southern end of Hartford Wood on the Beaulieu Estate. His wife, Laura (1867–1946) was the author of books on etiquette. Louise (1894–1961) and Rosemary (1905–1974) were his daughters.

WADLEY Frank (1866–1943)

Frank was the Superintendant of the Electric Light Station in Beaulieu.

WIDNELL Captain Henry Edward Rochfort (1893–1982)

Trained as a land agent, Captain Widnell served with the Seaforth Highlanders in the First World War but was discharged from the army on medical grounds in 1918. He joined the staff of the Beaulieu Estate as land agent on 7 September 1918 remaining at Beaulieu for the rest of his life. His support for Pearl after John Montagu's death was key in the management and maintenance of the estate. On his retirement, Captain Widnell was asked by Edward Montagu to compile an account of Beaulieu from the time when, in 1536, it was sold by Henry VIII to Thomas Wriothesley, 1st Earl of Southampton. *The Beaulieu Record* was published in 1973, a detailed history covering more than 400 years of lay ownership of the estate.

WOODROFFE Alice Joan (1910–1984)

The daughter of Pearl's Uncle Dick and his first wife, Sissie.

WOODROFFE Alice Maud *née* Townshend (1848–1906)

Pearl's maternal grandmother. *See* Chapter 1.

WOODROFFE Brigadier-General Charles Richard (1878–1965)

Pearl's 'Uncle Dick' was the second son of George and Alice Woodroffe. He joined the Royal Artillery and served in South Africa between 1899 and 1902 and went on to have a distinguished career in the army. A fluent Japanese speaker, he was attached to the Japanese army between 1907 and 1908. In 1917 he was appointed Assistant Adjutant and Quartermaster General. Between 1919 and 1921 he was once more in Japan as military attaché in Tokyo.

WOODROFFE Eleanor Mary 'Sissie', *née* Barlow Webb (1884–1918)

Sissie Eleanor married Charles Richard Woodroffe in 1909 but died in the 1918 influenza pandemic just days after the end of the First World War leaving two young children.

WOODROFFE George William Plukenett 'Diggles' (1842–1919)

Pearl's maternal grandfather. *See* Chapter 1.

WOODROFFE Islay Mary Cecil *née* Macdonald Moreton (1891–1968)

Islay was the second wife of Charles Richard Woodroffe. Pearl described him as looking 'too happy for words' when he brought Islay to meet her for the first time on 1 September 1921.

WOODROFFE John 'Jack' William (1916–1990)

The son of Pearl's Uncle Dick and his first wife, Sissie, Jack was one of the pages at Pearl's wedding in 1920. *See* Chapter 4.

1. House in the Wood
2. The Rings
3. Harford House
4. The Vineyards
5. Abbotswell
6. Palace House
7. Pan's Garden
8. Oxleys
9. House on the Shore
10. Littlemarsh

Culverley

Pennerly

Hartford

Hill Top

Leygreen

Beaulieu

Curtle

Swinesleys

Beufre

Home Farm

Otterwood

Ashen Wood

Keeping

Buckler's Hard

Monkshorn

Lodge

Clobb

Newlands

Bergerie

St Leonards

Salterns Hill

Beck

Buckersleys

Ginns

Beaulieu River

Sowley

Thorns

Park

Warren

Lepe >

The Solent

AFTERWORD

♦♦♦

Pearl's time as châtelaine to John Montagu was all too brief, but those few years of marriage had, as might be expected of two very energetic people, been packed with activity. She produced four children, became fully immersed in the estate and its people, travelled with John to many wonderful places and was embraced by her husband's family and wide circle of friends. This was to set the stage for the decades ahead, in which Pearl became the all-important continuity figure.

Although Pearl did not realise it whilst John was alive, she unwittingly became his understudy, absorbing knowledge of Beaulieu that would be essential in the years to come. It wasn't just factual knowledge but a sense of John's values as a father and Lord of the Manor. Best summed up in his motto 'I belong to Beaulieu, not Beaulieu belongs to me,' this fine ideal nevertheless had to be tempered by economic realities. The stock market crash in October 1929 didn't get a mention in Pearl's diary, but its consequences could not be avoided.

Talking to me about her diary many years later, my grandmother firmly declared that she had avoided any mention of her 'thoughts and fears'. She clearly regarded the recording or sharing of one's inner thoughts as inappropriate. Here was a woman who, rather than dwelling on future uncertainties, believed in getting on with the tasks to hand.

The financial and administrative burdens following John's death were very considerable. A lesser person might have withdrawn from both these and the role of family figurehead, preferring the easy route of selling up, or becoming an absentee landlord, but Pearl committed herself to bringing up her children at Beaulieu and ensuring the survival of the estate. Against the odds, and at a time when other estate owners were forced to sell land, the Beaulieu Estate remained intact to be inherited in 1951 by her son, my father, Edward Montagu.

What happened in the intervening 22 years is another story, but the legacy lives on in Beaulieu today, all of which flows from Pearl's little golden era with John which began in August 1920.

Montagu of Beaulieu

This map of the Beaulieu Estate was drawn in 1718, but the boundaries remained almost unchanged when Pearl first came to live in Beaulieu in 1920.

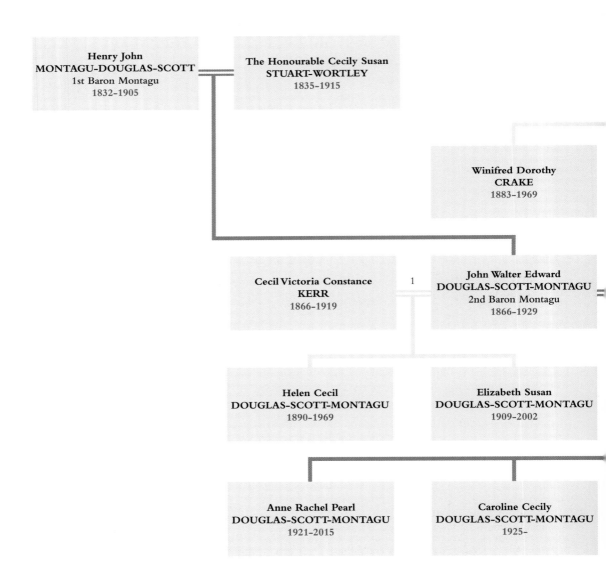

Vandeleur Benjamin
CRAKE JP
1816–1894

Henry John
MONTAGU-DOUGLAS-SCOTT
1st Baron Montagu
1832–1905

The Honourable Cecily Susan
STUART-WORTLEY
1835–1915

Winifred Dorothy
CRAKE
1883–1969

Cecil Victoria Constance
KERR
1866–1919

1

John Walter Edward
DOUGLAS-SCOTT-MONTAGU
2nd Baron Montagu
1866–1929

Helen Cecil
DOUGLAS-SCOTT-MONTAGU
1890–1969

Elizabeth Susan
DOUGLAS-SCOTT-MONTAGU
1909–2002

Anne Rachel Pearl
DOUGLAS-SCOTT-MONTAGU
1921–2015

Caroline Cecily
DOUGLAS-SCOTT-MONTAGU
1925–

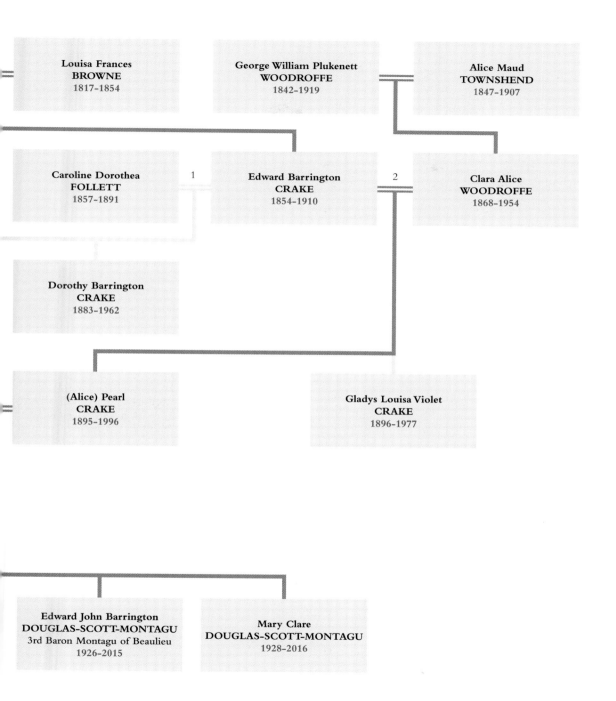

Louisa Frances
BROWNE
1817–1854

George William Plukenett
WOODROFFE
1842–1919

Alice Maud
TOWNSHEND
1847–1907

Caroline Dorothea
FOLLETT
1857–1891

1

Edward Barrington
CRAKE
1854–1910

2

Clara Alice
WOODROFFE
1868–1954

Dorothy Barrington
CRAKE
1883–1962

(Alice) Pearl
CRAKE
1895–1996

Gladys Louisa Violet
CRAKE
1896–1977

Edward John Barrington
DOUGLAS-SCOTT-MONTAGU
3rd Baron Montagu of Beaulieu
1926–2015

Mary Clare
DOUGLAS-SCOTT-MONTAGU
1928–2016

INDEX

♦♦♦

References to photographs are shown in **_bold italic_** type.